The Handbook of Convertibles

APPROPRIATE BALANCE
FINANCIAL SERVICES, INC.
11100 N.E. 8th St. Suite 370
Bellevue, WA 98004

The Handbook of Convertibles

Simon R. McGuire

New York Institute of Finance
New York London Toronto Sydney Tokyo Singapore

Library of Congress Cataloging-in-Publication Data
McGuire, Simon.
The handbook of convertibles/Simon McGuire.
  p.   cm.
Includes index.
ISBN 0-13-376062-6
1. Convertible securities. I. Title.
HG4651.M38 1990
332.63'2044—dc20
                                        90-43523
                                           CIP

This publication is designed to provide accurate and authoritative information in regard to the subject matter covered. It is sold with the understanding that the publisher is not engaged in rendering legal, accounting, or other professional service. If legal advice or other expert assistance is required, the services of a competent professional person should be sought.

*From a Declaration of Principles
Jointly Adopted by
a Committee of the American Bar Association
and a Committee of Publishers and Associations*

© 1991 by NYIF Corp.
A Division of Simon & Schuster
A Paramount Communications Company

All rights reserved. No part of this book may be reproduced in any form or by any means without permission in writing from the publisher

Printed in Great Britain

To Nicky and Rachel

Contents

	Preface		ix
	Acknowledgements		xi
Part I	**Introduction and definitions**		**1**
	Chapter 1	Introduction and definitions	3
Part II	**The issuer's perspective**		**13**
	Chapter 2	The rationale for issuing convertibles	15
	Chapter 3	Principal types of convertible	22
	Chapter 4	Convertible versus bond with equity warrants issue	39
	Chapter 5	Summary and conclusions	43
Part III	**The investor's perspective**		**45**
	Chapter 6	The rationale for investing in convertibles	47
	Chapter 7	Types of convertible	59
	Chapter 8	Pitfalls in convertible investing	68
	Chapter 9	Summary and conclusions	76
Part IV	**Convertible valuation**		**77**
	Chapter 10	Convertible valuation	79
Part V	**The principal markets**		**97**
	Chapter 11	Overview of the Euromarket	99
	Chapter 12	Overview of the US domestic market	117
	Chapter 13	Overview of the Swiss market	132
	Chapter 14	Overview of the Japanese domestic market	146
	Glossary		160
	Index		164

Preface

In recent years, interest in convertibles has increased considerably. From a relatively modest base in the 1970s, new issues of convertibles in the world's major capital markets have grown to the point where in 1989 almost US$100 billion was raised worldwide in this form. Growth in issuing has been matched by similar growth in investing: at the beginning of 1990, for example, the market value of outstanding convertibles in the world's major capital markets totalled almost US$500 billion. The number and types of investor now owning convertibles has also increased. One of the hallmarks of the 1980s, for example, was the considerable growth in dedicated convertible funds, i.e. funds whose sole mandate is to invest in convertibles. In the United States, their number has tripled or quadrupled in the last few years alone.

One might conclude from this that convertibles are a relatively new phenomenon, like so many other financial products of the 1980s. This is not so: convertibles have been used regularly by issuers and investors alike for at least a century. For example, US railroads were built partly from the proceeds of convertible financings. In fact, one can trace the origins of convertibles all the way back to the beginnings of corporate finance.

Why have convertibles been around for so long? Perhaps the major reason is that for both issuers and investors alike, convertibles offer benefits which traditional forms of capital (stocks and bonds) do not. For the issuer, convertibles offer the possibility of selling shares at a premium; for the investor, convertibles offer the combination of the income and capital preservation advantages of bonds with the long-run growth potential of stocks.

This book is divided into five parts. The first part introduces convertibles by providing a brief description of the principal merits of convertible securities together with definitions of the most commonly used terms. The second part looks at convertibles from the issuer's point of view. It is directed primarily at the financial staff of, and bankers to, companies faced with the need to raise capital from external sources. It explains why and in what circumstances a convertible issue makes sense. It reviews the different types of convertible that can be issued, and the advantages and disadvantages of each. It concludes by contrasting the merits of a convertible financing with a bond with equity warrants issue.

The third part looks at convertibles from the investor's perspective. It is directed primarily at individual investors and portfolio managers who are familiar with the merits of bond and stock investing, but who have little experience of convertibles. It explains how and in what circumstances investing in convertibles makes sense. It reviews the different types of convertible and their advantages and disadvantages relative to other forms of investment. It concludes by describing some of the pitfalls in convertible investing.

The fourth part provides a practical method of valuing convertibles which can be used without the need for complex computer valuation packages. The fifth part provides an overview of the four largest and most accessible convertible markets in the world: the Euromarket, and the domestic markets in Japan, Switzerland and the United States. It is intended for both issuers and investors alike and provides a brief overview of the principal characteristics of each market, and the types of convertible that are commonly available.

Acknowledgements

No-one can write a book like this without a great deal of help, and I am no exception. Many people helped me write it, and to each one I express my sincere thanks. Lawton Fitt, Kiyoshi Fukunaga, Mark Hantho, Sol Hartman, Mike Hintze, Heinrich Hirzel, Doug Howland, Shuichi Kondoh, Michael Watson and Sylvia Watson were all instrumental in creating parts of the book, either by supplying basic information, or by reviewing those sections of the book where their knowledge and experience greatly exceeded mine.

Peter Mallinson and Gary Williams used their considerable expertise in convertibles in painstakingly reviewing early drafts of the manuscript, and in making many helpful comments and suggestions which were incorporated in the final version. Remco Lenterman is the creator of many of the graphical illustrations, while Kelly Sandys typed (and retyped, and retyped, . . .) the manuscript with unceasing good humour.

There are also many colleagues at work who have helped indirectly; without their influence over the years I would never have been given the opportunity to write the book in the first place. The list is too long to mention them all, but Geoff Boisi, Michael Cohrs, Bob Conway, Eric Dobkin, John Downing, Paul Efron, Gene Fife, Henry James, Will Mesdag, David Silfen, Roy Smith, Bob Steel, Artur Walther, John Weinberg and Roy Zuckerberg have all had an impact in one way or another. To them and to all the others who have helped me, I am sincerely grateful.

Finally, my biggest debt of gratitude is due to my wife and family, to whom this book is dedicated, because without their patience, help and support during the many hours that it took to put the book together, I would never have been able to complete the task at all.

The material in this book is based upon information which the author believes to be reliable, but he does not represent that it is accurate or complete, and it should not be relied upon as such. Where opinions are expressed, they are the personal opinions of the author and do not necessarily represent those of any other person or organisation.

Part I

Introduction and definitions

Chapter I

Introduction and definitions

A convertible is part debt, part equity. For the investor, a convertible offers the safety of income and principal protection that debt offers, as well as the growth potential of equity. For the issuer, a convertible offers the possibility of selling stock at a premium, and the attraction of low cost debt in the period before it is converted. For both parties, a convertible is neither wholly debt, nor wholly equity. It is a true hybrid.

Convertibles come in many different forms. Some are more debt-like, others more equity-like. At one extreme, convertible preferred stock is the most equity-like of all convertible securities, while at the other extreme, zero coupon convertible bonds are the most debt-like. Convertible bonds (sometimes called convertible debentures) are far more common than convertible preferreds and come in many different forms: as a result, discussion of convertibles in this book relates mainly to convertible bonds.

Debt characteristics of convertibles

Fixed coupon

Most convertibles pay a fixed annual coupon while they are outstanding in the same way as straight bonds. The coupon is usually lower than that on the equivalent straight bond to reflect the value of the conversion option in the convertible.

Mandatory redemption

Most convertibles are mandatorily redeemed at final maturity in the same way as straight bonds. The redemption price is the convertible's par (redemption) value. The final redemption date occurs at any time from five to thirty years after issue date, depending on the market in which they are issued. In addition, some convertibles (particularly those offered in the US market) incorporate a sinking fund.

The convertible's guarantee of income and return of principal, together with the conversion option, offers the risk-averse investor a unique and attractive method of participating in the equity market. Capital preservation is ensured (provided the company remains solvent), while the conversion option also ensures that the benefits of any long-term growth in the share price are captured as well.

Events of default and rights of acceleration

Convertible bonds usually offer the same rights and remedies in the event of a missed coupon or principal payment that straight bonds typically incorporate. In particular, the investor has the right to declare a default and accelerate repayment of principal. No such right usually exists on convertible preferreds or common stock.

Ranking in liquidation

The convertible investor usually (but not always) ranks behind the straight bond investor, in front of equity investors in a liquidation of the company.

Optional redemption features

Issuer's option

Most convertibles are callable for redemption prior to final maturity at the issuer's option at any time. The call period usually starts within a few years of original issue date. Since the coupon is lower than that on straight debt, companies generally only exercise the call option to force investors to convert the bonds into equity. This is possible only when the company's share price has appreciated substantially so that the market value of the shares into which the bonds can be converted exceeds the redemption price of the bonds. Once the call is announced, there is normally a short period until the bonds are repaid, during which investors can make up their minds either to redeem the bonds or convert them into equity. Barring a precipitous decline in the company's share price during this period, it usually makes sense to convert. Sometimes the issuer's right to call can only be exercised if the company's share price has reached a pre-determined trigger level (provisional call); at other times, there are no such pre-conditions (absolute right of call).

Investor's option

Some convertibles offer the investor the right to redeem the bonds earlier than the stated maturity date (a put option). On some convertibles the put option is at a premium to par; on others, it is at par itself. In return for offering the put option, the coupon on the convertible is usually lower than normal and/or the conversion premium (defined below) is higher.

Event risk clause

An increasing number of convertibles, particularly those issued by US companies, protect the investor against unexpected takeover or merger activity in the same way that straight bonds do.

Equity characteristics of convertibles

All convertibles are convertible at the investor's option into a pre-determined number of shares. The conversion option can usually be exercised at any time or at specified points during the convertible's life. No money changes hands on exercise; rather, the investor exchanges the convertible bond for a specified number of shares.

The number of shares into which a convertible can be exchanged is called the conversion ratio. It is determined at the outset and is usually established so that the issue price of the convertible represents a premium to the market value of the shares into which it can be converted. This premium is called the conversion premium.

The conversion option ensures that the convertible investor can capture any benefits accruing to the stock investor, particularly the long-run growth potential of the stock. The convertible investor pays a premium over the stock price (the conversion premium) in order to obtain this; in return, the convertible investor also benefits from the capital preservation and income advantages of being one of the company's bondholders.

Market behaviour

Exhibit 1.1 illustrates the price performance of a typical convertible against changes in the underlying share price, and illustrates the principal attractions of convertibles for both issuers and investors: for the issuer, the possibility of selling shares at a premium; for the investor, the combination of long-term capital growth through growth in the underlying share price together with the safety (capital preservation) feature of bonds.

The share price at point C is the share price which would typically prevail at the launch of a convertible offering. At this point the convertible is worth more than the shares into which it is convertible because of the value of the conversion option. This is the principal reason why companies issue convertibles: the conversion option enables them potentially to sell shares at a premium to their market price.

The investment attractions of convertibles are illustrated when the company's share price appreciates over time towards point D. The convertible investor benefits because the convertible appreciates in value in line with the shares. The rate of increase in the convertible's value will not be as great as that of the underlying

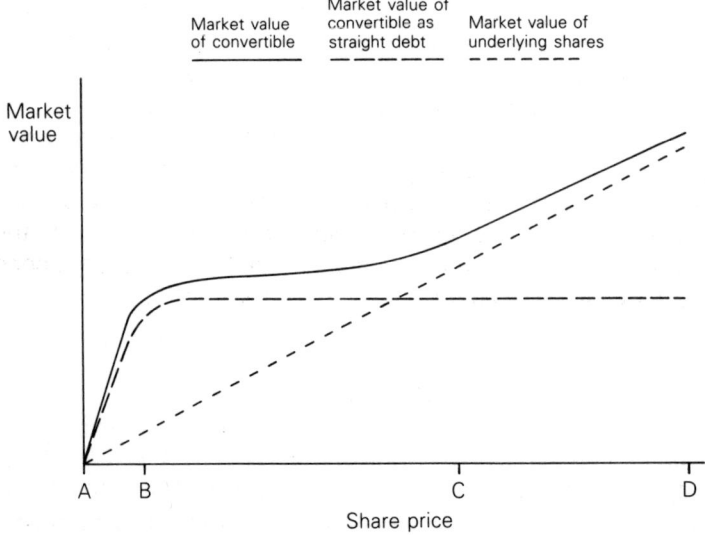

Exhibit 1.1 **Market value analysis**

shares because the conversion premium will erode; this is the sacrifice the convertible investor has to make in order to enjoy the downside protection benefits of the convertible. If the stock market declines or the company does not do so well, and the company's share price declines towards point B, the convertible investor is protected because the convertible's value is held up by its value as a straight bond. If the share price declines below point B towards point A, then this is probably because the company is in business or financial distress, in which case the value of the company's bonds, including the convertible, will also decline.

Definitions

Par value

The par value of a convertible is the convertible's redemption value as a bond at final maturity.

Bond value

The bond value of a convertible, sometimes called its investment value, is the value that the convertible would have if there were no conversion option, i.e. its value as a straight bond. As with straight bonds, a convertible's bond value changes in line with changes in interest rates. It can be calculated by discounting the future coupons and principal cash flows on the convertible at a discount rate equivalent to the straight debt rate of the company, adjusting if necessary for any call features on the convertible. The bond value differs from the par value to the extent that prevailing interest rates are higher or lower than the coupon on the convertible. If interest rates are higher than the coupon, the bond value will be lower than the par value, and vice versa.

Bond premium

The bond premium is the difference between the market value of the convertible and its bond value. It represents the incremental value to bond investors of the conversion option in the convertible.

Conversion ratio

The conversion ratio of a convertible is the number of shares into which each bond can be converted. For example, a $1,000 bond which can be converted into 20 shares of stock has a conversion ratio of 20. The conversion ratio is either defined in the prospectus, or is obtained by dividing the par value of the bond by the initial conversion price (defined below). The conversion ratio is fixed for the life of the convertible, except for adjustments as a result of the anti-dilution clause (defined below).

Conversion price

The conversion price is the price per share at which the bonds can be converted into shares of common stock, i.e. the value of the bonds divided by the number of shares per bond or conversion ratio. For example, a conversion price of $50 means a $1,000 bond can be converted into 20 shares of stock, calculated as follows:

$$\text{Number of shares of stock} = \frac{\$1,000}{\$50} = 20$$

The initial conversion price is established by the underwriters of the convertible at a premium to the prevailing market price of the shares. For example, the initial conversion price might be $50 when the shares were trading at $40. The initial conversion price is then used to determine the conversion ratio, according to the following formula:

$$\text{Conversion ratio} = \frac{\text{Issue price of bond}}{\text{Initial conversion price}}$$

$$= \frac{\$1,000}{\$50}$$

$$= 20 \text{ shares per } \$1,000 \text{ bond}$$

Unlike the conversion ratio, the conversion price may change

INTRODUCTION AND DEFINITIONS

during the life of the convertible. This will happen where there is a redemption or put option at a premium to the convertible's issue price. For example, if there is a put option at 120% of par, then the bonds will be worth $1,200 on the put date and the effective conversion price at this point will be $60 per share, not $50 as initially stated, calculated as follows:

$$\begin{aligned} \text{Conversion price} &= \frac{\text{Value of bond}}{\text{Conversion ratio}} \\ &= \frac{\$1,200}{20} \\ &= \$60 \text{ per share} \end{aligned}$$

If there are no put options, and the bonds are redeemed for the same value as they are issued, then the conversion price of a convertible will remain fixed in the same way as the conversion ratio. Unfortunately, many companies and their lawyers fail to recognise that conversion prices may change, with the result that many prospectuses relating to convertibles with premium put options state a fixed conversion price. The prudent investor will realise that it is the conversion ratio, not the conversion price, which remains fixed, and the only use for the stated conversion price is to calculate the conversion ratio.

Parity value

The parity value of a convertible is the market value of the shares into which it can be converted. Sometimes called the stock value or conversion value, the parity value is obtained by multiplying the conversion ratio by the share price. In the example, where the initial share price is $40, and the conversion ratio is 20, the initial parity value of each $1,000 bond is $800 or 80% of par, calculated as follows:

$$\begin{aligned} \text{Parity value} &= \text{Conversion ratio} \times \text{share price} \\ &= 20 \times \$40 \\ &= \$800 \\ &= 80\% \text{ of par} \end{aligned}$$

This compares with the convertible's issue price of $1,000: the convertible investor pays a premium of $200 over the market value of the shares in order to invest in the convertible.

Conversion premium

The conversion premium is the difference between the market value of a convertible and its parity value. In the example, if the market value of the convertible is $1,000, and its parity value is $800, the conversion premium is $200 or 25%, calculated as follows:

$$\text{Conversion premium} = \frac{\$1{,}000 - \$800}{\$800} = 25\%$$

The conversion premium is the value to stock investors of the higher income and downside protection offered by the convertible relative to its underlying shares.

Anti-dilution clause

Most convertibles protect the convertible investor in the event of actions on the company's part which might dilute their equity interest. These can include issues of equity at a discount (e.g. rights issues), scrip issues, subsidiary spin-offs, stock splits or one-time extraordinary dividends. The conversion ratio is usually adjusted upwards, pro rata the convertible investor's theoretical loss, in such events.

Types of convertible

Low premium convertible

A low premium convertible is one that is issued or trading with a low conversion premium (around 5%) and has a low coupon to match.

Conventional convertible

A conventional convertible has a traditional conversion premium (15 to 30%) and a higher coupon.

Premium put convertible

A premium put convertible is a convertible with an investor put option prior to final maturity, usually (but not always) at a premium to par. It can be a single premium put convertible (one-time put option), or a rolling or flexible premium put convertible (several put options at different points during the life of the bonds). Usually it has a lower coupon and/or a higher conversion premium than a conventional convertible. This is the issuer's compensation for offering the put option.

Zero coupon convertible

A zero coupon convertible is a convertible without a coupon. In the US market, zero coupon convertibles are more popularly referred to as LYONs (Liquid Yield Option Notes), after their creator, Merrill Lynch.

Convertible bonds

Convertible bonds are convertibles structured as debt securities, convertible into the company's equity. They are by far the most common type of convertible: low premium, conventional, premium put and zero coupon convertibles have all been issued as convertible bonds.

Convertible preferreds

Convertible preferreds are convertibles structured as preferred shares of equity, convertible into common stock. Except for an increase in yield, they have few of the debt characteristics of convertible bonds, with the result that they are much less popular with investors, and much rarer than convertible bonds. They are regularly issued in the US and UK domestic markets, but rarely issued elsewhere. The exception to this is the Euromarket, where some companies have issued convertible preferreds, although nearly always with the benefit of a debt guarantee so that the investor continues to benefit from debt-like protection when investing in the security.

Part II

The issuer's perspective

Chapter 2

The rationale for issuing convertibles

A convertible financing can be more advantageous for a company than an issue of either straight debt or straight equity. Most convertibles are highly likely to be converted; if they are converted they will enable the company to sell shares at a premium. Other types of convertible are more likely to be redeemed; if this occurs, the company will raise low cost debt instead.

In most circumstances, an issue of a conventional or rolling premium put convertible (described later) will be more advantageous than an issue of straight equity because the convertible is highly likely to be converted (i.e. almost certain to become straight equity) and because, once converted, it will have enabled the company to sell the shares at a price which is higher than that achieveable through a direct share issue. Correspondingly, in many circumstances an issue of a single premium put or zero coupon convertible (also described later) will be more advantageous than an issue of straight debt because the convertible has a much lower probability of conversion (i.e. a higher probability of being redeemed as straight debt instead) and because, once redeemed, it will have enabled the company to raise debt at a much lower cost than a straight debt issue.

The structure and applications of the types of convertible mentioned here are reviewed in more detail later. One point to note at this stage, however, is that the convertibles mentioned as an alternative to straight debt (single premium put and zero coupon convertibles) are not the same as those mentioned as an alternative to straight equity (conventional and rolling premium put convertibles). The principal difference between the two lies in the probability of conversion: those which are alternatives to equity are highly likely to be converted, whereas those which are alternatives to debt are much less so. As a consequence, one of the first decisions to make when deciding whether to issue a convertible is to determine whether debt or equity is required at the end of the day. If debt is desired, then one of the more debt-like convertibles should be considered; equally if equity is desired, one of the more equity-like convertibles should be considered.

It is also important to note that while in many circumstances a convertible will prove more advantageous than straight debt or straight equity, it will not be the case in all circumstances. Every company and every situation is unique; careful analysis of the company and its circumstances is advisable on each occasion, before determining that the generalisations presented here on the attractions of convertible financing are true.

Convertibles as an alternative to equity

A conventional or rolling premium put convertible can be more advantageous than a straight issue of shares, firstly because the convertible is almost certain to be converted and, secondly, because it enables the company to sell the shares at a higher price.

The first reason is illustrated as follows. A conventional convertible with a fifteen year maturity and a 20% conversion premium is certain to be converted if the company's share price rises by the conversion premium of 20% over fifteen years, equivalent to a compound annual growth rate of just 1.2%. Most companies achieve 20% growth in the share price in a considerably shorter time frame: there are very few for whom such growth in fifteen years is not virtually assured. As a consequence, a conventional convertible is almost certain to be converted into equity, and can therefore be viewed as an alternative method of raising equity.

A rolling premium put convertible also has a high probability of conversion, although slightly lower than that of a conventional convertible. The probability of conversion is examined in more detail later; the point to note at this stage, however, is that most rolling premium put convertibles can be structured so that the convertible will be converted provided the company's share price keeps pace with inflation during the life of the bond. Most companies would view the target of keeping their share price growing at inflation as more than attainable over the long run, with the consequence that these types of convertible are likely to be converted.

Exhibit 2.1 illustrates this situation graphically. It shows the effective conversion price (i.e. the share price at which a convertible investor would be indifferent between converting the bonds

THE RATIONALE FOR ISSUING CONVERTIBLES 17

and redeeming them) of a typical conventional convertible and a typical rolling premium put convertible plotted over time. Overlaid on top of the conversion prices is a graph of what happens to the company's share price if it grows at a compound annual rate of 5% (assumed to be equivalent to keeping pace with inflation). It can be seen that well before final maturity, the company's share price will have exceeded the conversion price of both types of convertible, with the result that they are certain to be converted.

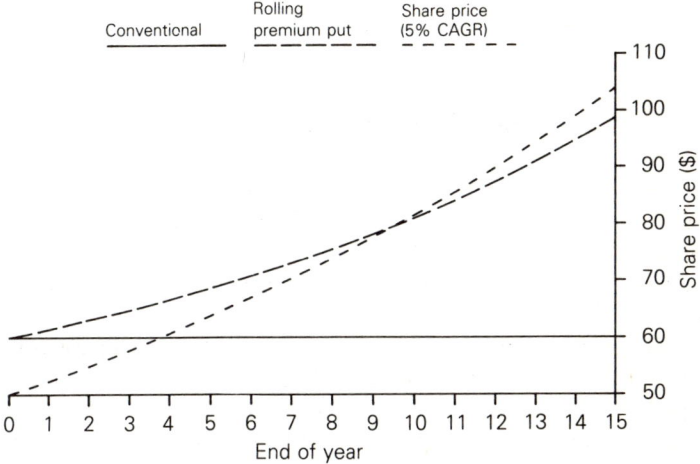

Exhibit 2.1 Analysis of conversion prices on various convertible structures

The second reason why both types of convertible can be more advantageous than a direct issue of shares is because they enable the company to sell the shares at a higher price. Shares sold through the mechanism of a convertible are sold at a premium to the market price; in contrast, shares sold directly to the market are priced either at the current market price or at a discount to it (which can be substantial in the case of a rights issue).

Some might argue that the premium obtained from the convertible is offset over time by the extra cost of paying coupons on the convertible, rather than dividends on the underlying shares; most convertibles carry coupons which are higher than the dividends on the underlying shares. However, this is usually not the case, because convertible coupons can be deducted for tax purposes, but dividends on shares cannot, and the incremental cost of the convertible coupons on a post-tax basis is usually small relative to the premium, with the result that companies are still 'ahead' if they issue shares through a convertible rather than directly.

One of the most compelling ways to illustrate the cost advantage of a convertible is to perform a cost of capital calculation. There are several different methods of calculating cost of capital, and no one method is accepted as universal. One of the simplest and most common methods is a model which projects the cash flows associated with the funding alternative (dividends in the case of equity, for example, or coupons and principal in the case of straight debt), if necessary assigns a terminal value to the funding alternative (the theoretical cost if the shares were repurchased in the case of equity, for example), and performs an internal rate of return calculation on the resulting cash flows using the initial proceeds of the funding alternative as the initial cash flow. The model makes an assumption about the future rate of growth in the company's share price and dividends in order to perform this calculation for share and convertible issues; this assumption is then varied in order to extract a range of different values for the company's cost of capital against a range of assumptions on future share price growth.

Exhibit 2.2 illustrates the results of this method for a typical company considering three different funding alternatives: straight debt, a conventional convertible and straight equity. The graph illustrates a number of points, the first of which is intuitively obvious:

1. For most companies, straight debt is the cheapest form of capital. Straight debt is cheaper than either equity or a convertible provided the company's share price grows at more than 4% per annum. Most companies usually generate share price growth considerably in excess of this in the long run, which is why straight debt is the cheapest form of capital.
2. From a cost perspective, a conventional convertible has more in common with straight equity than straight debt. The graph showing the cost of the convertible tracks that of straight equity much more than that of straight debt.
3. A conventional convertible costs less than straight equity. This illustrates the cost advantage of a convertible, and reflects both the premium inherent in a convertible and the incremental cost of the coupons.

Exhibit 2.2 suggests that from a cost perspective, the company should be considering a conventional convertible only if it needs equity; and that provided it can tolerate the extra debt on the balance sheet which the convertible would represent until it is converted (which Exhibit 2.1 indicates is not likely to be long), the convertible is a more cost efficient method of raising that equity.

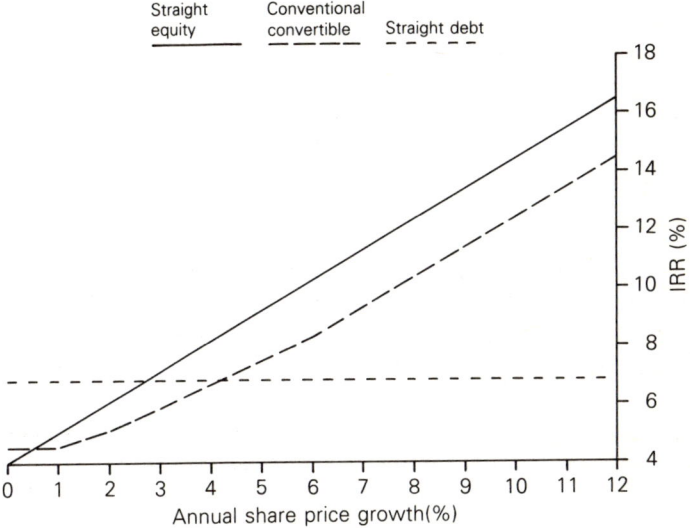

Exhibit 2.2 After tax cost of capital

Of course, not every company will be in the same position as the company in Exhibit 2.2. A word of caution is again appropriate here: every company and every convertible is unique and the generalisations presented here will not apply in all circumstances. It is quite possible, for example, that if the company in question had a low dividend yield and no ability to shelter convertible coupons for tax purposes, the incremental cost of paying the coupons on the convertible will more than offset the premium, with the result that the convertible will be more expensive than straight equity. For companies not in this position, however, a convertible is likely to be more advantageous than an issue of shares because it will enable the company to sell shares at a higher price. The convertible's only drawback is that it may not get converted; for most companies in most circumstances, however, this is unlikely.

Convertibles as an alternative to debt

For companies in low growth industries, single premium put or zero coupon convertibles can sometimes be more advantageous than straight debt because they have a lower probablity of conversion (i.e. a higher probability of redemption), and, if redeemed, they enable the company to raise debt at a lower cost than straight debt.

Exhibit 2.3 illustrates the lower probability of conversion by plotting the effective conversion prices of both types of convertible over time, and overlaying on top a graph of what happens to the company's share price if it grows at 5% per annum, i.e. keeps pace with inflation. It can be seen that very much in contrast to the convertibles illustrated in Exhibit 2.1, at no point does the share price exceed the conversion price of either convertible. In consequence, neither type of convertible will be converted if the company's share price just keeps pace with inflation. Growth substantially in excess of inflation will be required for this.

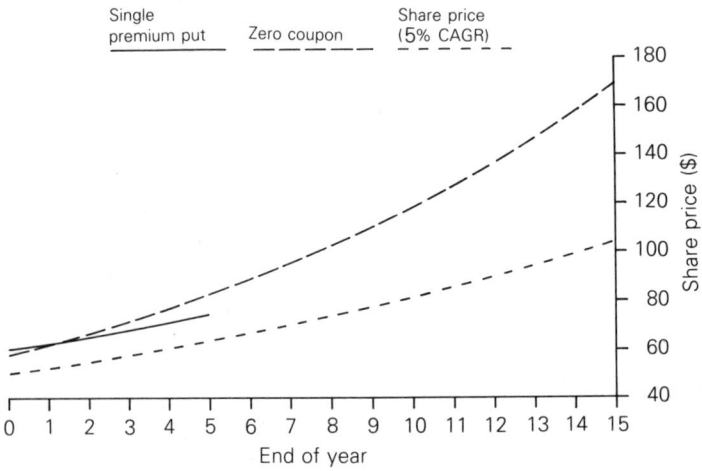

Exhibit 2.3 Analysis of conversion prices on various convertible structures

This is a very different scenario to that which prevails for the two equity-type convertibles considered earlier. Since there is a very real prospect that a single premium put or a zero coupon convertible will be redeemed instead of being converted, issuance of one or other can be viewed as an alternative to issuing debt, rather than equity. If a single premium put or zero coupon convertible is redeemed, its cost will be significantly below the cost of straight debt. In order to determine whether issuing the convertible made sense, it would be appropriate to weigh the savings against the likelihood of conversion. For companies in high growth industries, even a single premium put or zero coupon convertible is likely to be converted, because the company's share price may still outgrow the conversion price. As a consequence, for companies in this category even these types of convertibles can be considered as an alternative to an issue of equity.

Chapter 3

Principal types of convertible

So far, all that has been demonstrated is that issuing some convertibles can be more advantageous than issuing straight equity because the convertibles are almost certain to be converted and the shares are sold at a higher price. Other types of convertible can be issued instead of straight debt because there is a greater likelihood that the convertible will be redeemed instead of converted, resulting in significant cost savings relative to straight debt. This chapter reviews in more detail the different types of convertible, the reasons why each type has a different probability of conversion, and the circumstances in which it is appropriate to use them.

There are five principal convertible structures in use around the world: ranked by descending order of probability of conversion into equity, they are as follows:

	Probability of conversion into equity
Low premium convertible	Very high
Conventional convertible	High
Rolling premium put convertible	Moderately high
Single premium put convertible	Moderately low
Zero coupon convertible	Low

The low premium convertible has the highest probability of conversion, but the lowest conversion premium. The conventional convertible offers a higher conversion premium, but at the risk of a slightly reduced probability of conversion. The rolling premium put offers an even higher and rising effective conversion premium, but at the risk of a further reduced probability of conversion. The single premium put offers substantial savings relative to straight debt rates but at the risk of a moderately low probability of conversion into equity. The zero coupon convertible offers similar or greater savings relative to straight debt and an even lower probability of conversion into equity, but with the drawback of reduced marketability.

The best way of illustrating the differences between the five types of convertible is to consider how they would apply to a specific example. Suppose that ABC Company is a typical company with a profitable business, a strong balance sheet (single A credit characteristics), and a market capitalisation of $3 billion. Its shares trade at $50 each, and pay a dividend of $2 per annum, to yield 4%. ABC's medium (five years) and long-term (fifteen years) borrowing costs are 10% and 10½% respectively. Each type of convertible, and its applications for ABC, is reviewed below.

Low premium convertible

For most companies, a low premium convertible is almost certain to be converted. Relative to a direct issue of shares, it offers a modest premium on price, and, in the period before conversion, a lower servicing cost (the post-tax cost of paying coupons is usually lower than that of paying dividends).

Low premium convertibles are the most common form of convertible issued by Japanese companies, either in the Japanese domestic market or in the Euromarket. Issuance by Western companies up to now has been limited. Suppose the principal terms for a low premium convertible issue by ABC were as follows:

Amount	$200 million
Coupon	5%
Maturity	Fifteen years
Conversion premium	5%
Issue price	100%
Call options	Non-callable for three years. Thereafter callable at any time at a small, declining, premium to par.

If the bonds are converted, ABC effectively sells stock at a 5% premium to the current market price. Given the current market price of $50, this implies a conversion price of $52.50. In return for this premium, ABC (i) pays the investor a coupon of 5%, which represents a premium of approximately 1% to the cost of paying dividends on the underlying shares, and (ii) agrees to redeem the bonds at face value at final maturity in 15 years if they are not converted beforehand. In addition, ABC retains the option to call the bonds for early redemption at any time from the end of the third year onwards.

One of the first features to note about the convertible is that although the coupon on the bonds is higher than the initial dividend cost of the shares, on a post-tax basis it may well be lower, turning an apparent drawback of the convertible into an additional advantage. For example, at a 35% tax rate, the post-tax cost of the bonds will be 3.3%, which is lower than the 4.0% cost of paying dividends. The savings from the convertible would increase over time as dividends on the shares increased. The second feature to note is that the convertible is almost certain to be converted. All that is required is that ABC's share price rise above the conversion price, i.e. slightly more than 5%, at some point during the life of the convertible. If conversion does not take place spontaneously beforehand, then it will definitely do so at final maturity because the value of the shares which would be issued upon conversion will exceed the value of redemption.

Example

The number of shares issuable upon conversion, called the conversion ratio, is calculated by dividing the par value of the bond ($1,000) by the initial conversion price ($52.50) as follows:

$$\text{Conversion ratio} = \frac{\$1{,}000}{\$52.50} = 19.048$$

If ABC's share price at final maturity were $55, the value of the shares issuable upon conversion would be $55 × 19.048 = $1,047.62. This exceeds the bond redemption value of $1,000, so that investors would convert the bonds, rather than allow the company to redeem them. Conversely if ABC's share price were unchanged at final maturity, then the value of the shares issuable upon conversion ($50 × 19.048 = $952.38) would be lower than the redemption value of the bonds, so that investors would allow the company to redeem them. The point of difference for the investor between converting and redeeming is the conversion price of $52.50. If the company's share price at final maturity is above this, then investors will convert. If it is not, then investors will redeem.

Of course, conversion may well occur earlier than final maturity, because ABC retains the ability to call the bonds. If ABC calls the bonds when its share price is above the conversion price (adjusted upwards, if necessary, to reflect any call premium on the bonds), investors will be economically better off converting rather than redeeming, so the bonds will be converted. Since ABC can call the bonds at any time from the end of the third year onwards, this gives ABC tremendous flexibility to force conversion: conversion can effectively be forced at any time between the end of year three and year fifteen provided ABC's share price rises 5% at some point during this period. In the worst analysis, all that is required is that ABC's share price rise a total of 5% by final maturity, equivalent to a compound growth rate of 0.3% per annum. There are very few companies for whom this is not an easily attainable target, which is why conversion of a low premium convertible is virtually assured.

Conventional convertible

The low premium convertible represents a method of selling equity at a premium with a very low risk of non-conversion. However the premium offered is modest: only 5%, which for many companies is insufficient reward for undertaking a convertible financing. For a negligible increase in conversion risk, a conventional convertible overcomes this drawback by offering a higher premium, usually between 15% and 25%.

Conventional convertibles are the most common type of convertible issued by Western companies and are in use in most major domestic convertible markets outside Japan, as well as the Euromarket. The principal terms for a conventional issue by ABC are set out below:

Amount	$200 million
Coupon	7%
Maturity	Fifteen years
Conversion premium	20%
Issue price	100%
Call options	Non-callable for three years. Thereafter callable at any time, at a small, declining, premium to par.

If the bonds are converted, the company will sell stock at a 20% premium, i.e. $60, to the current market price. In return for this benefit, the company pays the investor a 7% coupon and agrees to redeem the bonds in fifteen years if they are not converted beforehand. In addition, the company retains the right to redeem the bonds at any time from the end of the third year onwards.

A conventional convertible has a high probability of conversion into equity – the company's stock price must appreciate by only 20% over fifteen years, equivalent to a compound growth rate of 1.2% per annum, to ensure conversion – and as a consequence is widely used as an alternative to a straight equity issue. Exhibit 2.1 illustrates this point for ABC – the convertible depicted is a conventional convertible issued by ABC. One slight drawback of a conventional convertible is that the premium does not reflect the extra cost of paying the coupons on the convertible relative to the dividends on the underlying shares. Even on a post-tax basis, the cost of the coupons is likely to be higher (for example, at a 35% tax rate, ABC's post-tax convertible cost is 4.6%) and this will continue to be so until dividends on the underlying shares have increased to the point where they exceed the coupons.

There are a number of methods for reflecting this extra cost and calculating the true premium or cost advantage of a convertible. One method uses the cost of capital model described earlier and is illustrated in Exhibit 2.2. It shows that from a cost of capital perspective, a conventional convertible is less expensive than straight equity, despite the extra cost of paying the coupons. Another simpler method of illustrating the same point is as follows: suppose the company's share price and dividends grow at 10% per annum, and the bonds are converted into equity at the end of the third year. This would happen if the company chose to call the bonds for early redemption at the first possible opportunity, i.e. at the end of year three. Because the company's share price at this point ($66.55 at a 10% growth rate) exceeds the conversion price, the bonds would be converted. The true premium of the convertible would then be reduced to 17%, which is the stated premium less the net present value cost of the difference, on a post-tax basis, between the coupons on the bonds and the dividends on the shares, calculated as follows:

Year	Pre-tax	Coupons per $1,000 bond Tax savings[1]	Post-tax (A)	Dividends saved on underlying shares (B)	Incremental cash-flow cost of convertible (A − B)
1	$70	$(24.50)	$45.50	$33.33[2]	$12.17
2	70	(24.50)	45.50	36.67	8.83
3	70	(24.50)	45.50	40.33	5.17

Net present value of incremental cash flow cost at 10% discount rate	=	$22.25 per $1,000 bond
	=	$1.34 per underlying share
Stated conversion price	=	$60 per share
Less incremental cash flow cost of convertible	=	$1.34
True conversion price	=	$58.66, equivalent to a 17% premium.

Notes: [1] 35% assumed tax rate.
[2] Conversion ratio (16.667 shares per bond) times dividend ($2 per share initially), growing at a 10% rate.

Rolling premium put convertible

A rolling premium put convertible is identical to a conventional convertible in all but three respects:

1. The coupon is lower.
2. The conversion price rises during the life of the bond.
3. At several points during the life of the bonds, the investor has the right to redeem the bonds early, at a premium to par.

For some companies (e.g. US issuers) there is a fourth difference: the investor's yield to put (which is higher than the coupon) is tax deductible as interest expense, rather than just the coupon.

Relative to a conventional or low premium convertible, the principal advantages of a rolling premium put convertible are lower cash flow costs and a higher, rising, effective conversion price. If the bonds are converted, the company effectively sells stock at a higher price than is possible through a conventional or low premium convertible. The principal disadvantages are the put risk and the slightly lower probablity of conversion, although the latter is still sufficiently high to make it more than likely that the convertible will be converted.

The rolling premium put convertible is common in the Euromarket, where it was first introduced in early 1988. Its use has not yet spread to other convertible markets, although it is expected to do so. Principal terms for an issue by ABC are as follows:

Amount	$200 million
Coupon	5%
Maturity	Fifteen years
Conversion premium	20% initially, rising thereafter
Call options	1. On investor put dates, at put price.
	2. At any other time at a small declining premium to par, but in the first five years only if the share price has appreciated to 130% of initial conversion price. 'Test' percentage increased thereafter in line with accretion in put prices.
Put options	After five years, and annually thereafter, at prices to give the investor a 7½% yield to put. The prices would be 114.5% (end of year 5), 118.1% (end of year 6), 122.0% (end of year 7) etc.

The rolling premium put convertible is a complex security which at first glance is difficult to understand. Patience and persistence in trying to comprehend it can, however, be rewarding, because for some companies it will prove to be the most attractive alternative. Each of its major features (rising conversion price, lower cash flow cost, the put risk, and the probability of conversion) is reviewed in more detail below.

Rising conversion price

The conversion price of a convertible security is defined as the price the investor effectively pays the issuer per share of stock at the point when the bonds are converted. If conversion were to take place on day one for example, this would be the issue price of the bonds divided by the number of shares per bond (or conversion ratio). In ABC's case, for example, the initial conversion price would be $60.

Over time, the effective price paid by the investor to convert the rolling premium put rises. However, the investor does not pay the issuer any extra cash. Instead, the price rises because the issuer pays a lower than normal coupon. In ABC's case the coupon on a rolling premium put would be 5%, compared with 7% in a conventional convertible. ABC therefore saves 2% per annum by issuing the rolling premium put.

Coupon savings for the issuer represent income foregone by the investor: the investor gives up income to the issuer in order to own the rolling premium put. While not a transfer of cash, the savings are a transfer of economic value from investor to issuer. The longer the bonds are outstanding the more the investor foregoes and the greater the benefit derived by the issuer. This is reflected in the rising effective conversion price. Of course, the issuer's savings are conditional upon the investor ultimately converting the bonds. If the investor were to redeem the bonds instead, then the issuer would have to pay back all the savings accrued to that point, plus additional back interest, to give the investor a premium on redemption which produces the yield to put (7½% in ABC's case), which is higher than the coupon on a conventional convertible. However, if the investor converts, the risk of redemption is removed, and the issuer retains the savings in perpetuity.

In some countries (e.g. the United States), there is another source of value derived by the issuer which also serves to increase the effective conversion price. Where the yield to put, rather than the coupon, is the interest expense deduction for tax purposes, the tax deductions on a rolling premium put are greater than those on a conventional convertible. ABC, for example, can deduct 7½% per annum on a rolling premium put compared with 7% per annum on a conventional convertible. Extra tax deductions save taxes and, again, the longer the bonds are outstanding, the greater the total taxes saved.

From the investor's perspective, the conversion price rises because the price at which the investor is indifferent between converting or redeeming the bonds rises throughout the life of the security. In contrast, the conversion price is fixed for life in a conventional convertible. For example, in ABC's case the effective conversion price of the rolling premium put on day one is $60. By the end of year five, however, it has risen to just under $69, or a premium of 37% over the share price at launch, calculated as follows:

End of year five redemption value of bonds	=	Cash value of put option
	=	114.5% of par
	=	$1,145 per $1,000 bond
Number of shares per $1,000 bond	=	Conversion ratio
	=	16.667
Effective conversion price	=	Effective indifference price between converting and redeeming
	=	$\dfrac{\text{Redemption value of bond}}{\text{Number of shares per bond}}$
	=	$\dfrac{\$1{,}145}{16.667}$
	=	$68.71

The investor will only convert the rolling premium put if the share price is above $69 at the end of year five. This results in an effective conversion premium of 37%, not the stated premium of 20% prevailing at launch.

The effective conversion price also rises from an accounting perspective. Under the most conservative method of accounting, the bonds are accrued in the balance sheet from par initially up to the put price in each year. The interest expense in the income statement is the yield to put calculated on the accreted value of the bonds, rather than the coupon; the difference between this and the coupon is the amount of accrual added to the bonds each year. Upon conversion, the accreted value of the bonds is transferred from debt to shareholders' equity. Since the number of shares per bond is fixed, the effective transfer price (being the accreted value of the bonds divided by the number of shares per bond) rises in line with the accretion in the bonds. In ABC's case, for accounting purposes the rolling premium put would have the following conversion prices:

End of year	Effective conversion price ($)	Effective conversion premium (%)
0	60.00	20.0
5	68.71	37.4
10	81.22	62.4
15	99.18	98.4

This is illustrated graphically in Exhibit 2.1.

The implications of a rising conversion price for the issuer are significant. Relative to a conventional convertible where the conversion price is fixed, the rolling premium put can be viewed as being less dilutive from an economic perspective, since shares issued upon conversion are effectively sold at increasingly higher prices. This makes the rolling premium put attractive to companies whose shareholders are particularly focused on minimising economic dilution of their ownership in the company.

Cash flow savings

The other principal advantage of a rolling premium put over a conventional convertible is its lower cash flow cost. In ABC's case the annual cash flow cost pre-tax would be $10 million for a rolling premium put (being 5% of $200 million) versus $14 million (7% of $200 million) for a conventional convertible. In countries where the yield to put is tax deductible (e.g. the United States), the savings are enhanced on a post-tax basis, because of the greater tax deductions. In ABC's case the rolling premium put would cost approximately one-half that of the conventional convertible:

Conventional convertible	
Pre-tax interest cost	$14.0m
Less: tax at 35% of coupon cost	(4.9)
Net cash flow cost	$9.1m
Rolling premium put	
Pre-tax interest cost	$10.0m
Less: tax at 35% of yield to put (7½% of $200 million)	(5.3)
Net cash flow cost	$4.7m

In some cases, the cash flow cost of the rolling premium put can also be lower than the cost of paying dividends on the shares underlying the bonds. In ABC's case the company would actually save cash flow by issuing a rolling premium put rather than issuing shares directly as follows:

Principal amount of bonds	$200.0m
Equivalent number of shares (16.667 per $1,000 bond)	3.3m
Cash flow cost of paying dividends ($2 per share)	$6.7m post-tax
Cash flow cost of rolling premium put	$4.7m post-tax
Cash flow savings from issuing rolling premium put	$2.0m post-tax

Furthermore, the savings from issuing the rolling premium put will increase to the extent that the company increases dividends in the future. Over time the combination of the rising conversion price and low cash flow cost make the rolling premium put an attractive alternative to a conventional convertible and a direct issue of equity. Provided the rolling premium put converts, the shares issued will have been sold at a higher price and, in the period before conversion, a lower cash flow cost than shares issued through a conventional convertible or directly to the market.

The put risk

The one principal drawback of the rolling premium put is the put risk. In contrast to a conventional convertible, where the investor has to wait as much as fifteen years to get his money back, the investor has an option to redeem a rolling premium put after only five years. Furthermore, the redemption price is at a premium to the bond's issue price. This, potentially, is a material disadvantage for issuers relative to a conventional convertible and is apparently inconsistent with the principal objective of a conventional or rolling premium put convertible financing, namely that of raising permanent equity capital. Permanent capital is not usually redeemable at the investor's option so soon!

In order to overcome this drawback, the put option on a rolling premium put is repeated periodically (for example, at the end of each of the following years). The prices of successive puts are established so as to give the investor an economic incentive, on any particular put date, to continue holding bonds past the put date. This is achieved by setting the put price level so that the minimum return between any two put dates is comparable to the return on straight bonds of an equivalent maturity. This gives the investor a worst case return comparable to that of straight bonds and a best case return which could be much higher, should the conversion option become more attractive. As a result, investors should continue to hold unconverted bonds past each put date.

The price and date of each put option can be established either at the time of the initial offering (as in ABC's case), or just before each preceeding put date. In the latter case, called a 'flexible rolling put convertible', only the first put price and date would be established at launch: the second put price would be determined just before the first put date on the basis of market conditions prevailing just before the first put date; the third put price would be established just prior to the second put date; and so on.

If theory translates into practice, the rolling premium put will remain outstanding until final maturity, unless previously converted. The issuer bears only two risks: the first is that interest rates rise, making the minimum yield between puts unattractive, so that the issuer has to increase the coupon or yield to put above that originally offered in order to restore the investor's incentive not to put; and the second is that there will not be such a material adverse change in the company's business prospects that nothing induces the investor to continue holding. As a consequence, companies who do not view a material downturn in their business prospects as likely, and who are willing to take the risk of having to 'bribe' the investor if interest rates rise, can view the rolling premium put as being a long-term instrument.

The likelihood of conversion

Provided the bonds remain outstanding, and provided the bonds are structured with a relatively low rate of accretion (i.e. the difference between the yield to put and the coupon is small enough so that the rate of increase in the put prices is not significant), a rolling premium put has a relatively high probability of conversion into equity. In ABC's case, to avoid the first put risk altogether, ABC's share price would need to appreciate by 37% over the five year period, equivalent to a compound growth rate of 6.6% per annum, or slightly in excess of inflation.

If this target were not met, and provided (i) interest rates had not changed in such a way as to necessitate an increase in the following put prices, and (ii) investors continued to hold the bonds until final maturity instead of putting, ABC's share price would need to appreciate by the effective conversion premium prevailing at final maturity, i.e. a total of 98.4% over fifteen years to ensure conversion. This is equivalent to a 4.7% compound annual growth rate. In other words, provided ABC's share price keeps pace with inflation, conversion of the rolling premium put is ensured.

The likelihood of conversion is enhanced through the call options which offer the issuer the ability to eliminate the put risk altogether by forcing the investor to convert. The typical call is a provisional call and works as follows. Provided the company's share price reaches a pre-determined level or trigger price for a short period (usually twenty to thirty days), the company can call the bonds for early redemption. The trigger price in the first five years is usually 130% of the initial conversion price. This is high enough so that not only does the market value of the shares into which the bonds can be converted substantially exceed the call price (thereby ensuring investors will convert when the call is announced), but also the investor has a reasonable capital gain after conversion. At the end of the first five years, the trigger price is usually adjusted upwards annually in line with the accretion in the put prices.

In ABC's case the trigger price in the first five years would be $78, being 130% of the initial conversion price. If ABC's share price reached this point, then ABC could call the bonds, and investors would convert rather than surrender to the call, because the value of the shares which would be issued upon conversion would exceed the value of the bond redemption:

Value of shares issued upon conversion (16.667 shares per bond at $78 per share)	=	$1300
Value of redemption (100% plus call premium and accrued interest of, say, 2½%)	=	$1025

This ability to call the bonds for early redemption is available to the issuer throughout the life of a rolling premium put convertible and enables the issuer to eliminate the put risk altogether, provided its share price appreciates.

Single premium put convertible

A single premium put convertible has more debt-like characteristics than all the other types of convertible hitherto considered because it has a much lower probability of conversion. Although many companies in the past have issued single premium put convertibles with a view to raising equity, it is more appropriate to use such an instrument as an alternative to debt. Companies that want to raise equity using a premium put structure are better advised to issue a rolling premium put instead.

Single premium put convertibles hae been issued in the past by many Western and Japanese companies, and are common in the Euromarket, Swiss and US domestic markets. Prior to the creation of the rolling premium put in early 1988, most single premium puts were issued with a view to raising equity. As will be illustrated, this is often a risky strategy because there is a reasonably high likelihood that the single premium put will be redeemed. Used as an alternative to debt, a single premium put is the same as a rolling premium put except that:

1. The put option is one-time, and is not repeated.
2. The coupon is lower, and the put price (and yield to put) is higher, in order to increase the probability of redemption.

Principal terms for an issue by ABC would be as follows:

Amount	$200 million
Coupon	4%
Maturity	Fifteen years
Conversion premium	20% initially, rising thereafter

Call options	Callable at any time at a small declining premium to par, but in the first five years, only if the share price has appreciated to 130% of the initial conversion price
Put option	At the end of year five, at 123.5%, to yield 8% to the investor.

It can be seen that the coupon and yield to put are lower and higher, respectively, than the coupon and yield to put on the rolling premium put described earlier. Although ABC could have issued a single premium put on the same terms as the rolling premium put, the terms have been altered in order to reduce the probability of conversion. (The yield to put is also higher to compensate the investor for the reduced coupon.) The reason why the probability of conversion is reduced is illustrated as follows. On the put date, the investor has to determine whether to hold, convert or redeem the bonds. Holding is unlikely in almost all circumstances, owing to the low coupon, long remaining life and lack of call protection on the bonds. There is, therefore, usually a 'sudden death' decision to redeem or convert. This is illustrated graphically in Exhibit 2.3 by plotting the effective conversion price of a single premium put only as far as the put date, rather than all the way to final maturity. Conversion will only take place if the value of the underlying shares exceeds the cash value of the put. Clearly, the higher the put price, the higher the cash value of the put and the higher the point of indifference for the investor between converting and putting. In ABC's case conversion would only happen if ABC's share price were to exceed $74.10, calculated as follows:

Cash value of put (123.5% per $1,000 bond)	$1,235.00
Number of underlying shares	16.667
Equivalent put value per share	$74.10

If ABC's share price were above $74.10, investors would convert; equally if it were below $74.10, they would redeem.

It can be seen that the point of indifference for the investor between converting and redeeming a single premium put is higher than it is at the same date for the rolling premium put: $74.10 versus $68.71 in ABC's case. Furthermore, were ABC to reduce the coupon and increase the yield to put on the single premium put still further, the put price would rise above 123.5%, and the point of indifference would increase even more. As it is,

ABC's share price would have to appreciate from $50 initially to $74.10 in five years' time, a 48% increase, equivalent to a compound annual growth rate of 8.2%, for the investor to want to convert.

Most companies might view such growth as being achievable over a long time horizon but would have much less confidence of being able to achieve it over a five year period. For companies in this position, there is a moderately high risk of the single premium put being redeemed, instead of converted, which is why it is more appropriate to use it as an alternative to debt. If redemption instead of conversion does occur, then the company will have raised debt at substantial savings relative to straight debt rates. In ABC's case, for example, the cost of debt would equal the yield to put of 8% plus amortisation of front end fees and expenses. Ignoring the latter for ease of comparison, this represents savings of 200 basis points relative to ABC's straight debt rate of 10%.

If, on the other hand, redemption does not happen, and the bonds are converted, then ABC will sell stock at an effective premium of 48% (the effective conversion premium rises for the same reasons as the premium rises on a rolling premium put), which is much higher than the stated initial conversion premium of 20%. Viewed in this fashion, a single premium put used as an alternative to a straight debt issue could be a 'win-win' security. It has a moderately high probability of being redeemed as debt, in which case the company will make substantial savings (200 basis points in ABC's case). Alternatively it will be converted, in which case the company will sell equity at a substantial premium (48% in ABC's case).

Zero coupon convertible

A zero coupon convertible (sometimes referred to as a Liquid Yield Option Note or LYON) is the most debt-like of all convertibles. Structurally, it is similar to a rolling premium put, except that:

1. The coupon is zero.
2. The bonds are issued at a steep discount to par, and redeemed on final maturity at par.

Zero coupon convertibles are in common use in the US domestic market. They are also occasionally used in the Swiss market as well, where they are structured as par priced bonds with optional redemption at a premium to par, rather than as deep discount securities redeemable at par. Principal terms for an issue by ABC structured in the US fashion would be as follows:

Amount	$400 million
Issue price	34%, to yield 7½% to maturity
Net proceeds	$136 million
Coupon	Zero
Maturity	Fifteen years
Conversion premium	15% initially, rising thereafter
Call options	Non-callable for three years. Callable thereafter at accreted value provided share price is a specified percentage of initial conversion price.
Put options	After five years at accreted value, i.e. 48½%, and periodically thereafter to yield 7½%.

The zero coupon convertible is the most debt-like of all convertible securities because the 'hurdle' rate of growth in the company's share price to ensure conversion, rather than redemption, is the highest. Investors are unlikely to convert before the first put date, even if there is a substantial yield pick-up offered by the underlying shares, because to do so would be to forego forever the downside protection offered by the put option. As a consequence, the zero coupon convertible is likely to be outstanding at least until the first put date, and the rate of share price growth required to ensure conversion at this point is higher than for any other type of convertible. In ABC's case the share price would need to appreciate by 64% over the next five years, equivalent to a 10.4% compound annual growth rate, to ensure conversion. This is calculated as follows:

Initial conversion price (15% premium to $50)	$57.50 (A)
Issue proceeds per $1,000 bond	$340.00 (B)
Conversion ratio (B÷A)	5.913 shares (C)
End of year five put value per $1,000 bond	$485.00 (D)
Effective conversion price on put date (D÷C)	$82.02
Effective conversion premium	64%

The effective conversion price over time for ABC's convertible is illustrated in Exhibit 2.3.

In a sense it can be argued that the zero coupon convertible takes the single premium put convertible to its logical limit by reducing the coupon to zero. Instead of increasing the yield to put to compensate the investor, however, the initial conversion premium is reduced instead. The yield to put is also made as low as possible in order to maximise the company's savings on straight debt rates. In ABC's case the cost of debt if the convertible is redeemed is lower than that of the single premium put (7½% versus 8%). As a consequence, from the perspective of using a convertible as an alternative to debt, the zero coupon convertible is the optimal security. It has the lowest probability of conversion and offers the most savings relative to straight debt rates if redeemed (250 basis points in ABC's case). If on the other hand it converts, it will result in the company selling stock at the highest premium (64% in ABC's case if conversion occurs after five years).

The zero coupon convertible's only drawback is that there is limited investor appetite. The only established market at present is in the United States, which effectively prevents many non-US companies from issuing them (because of the hurdle of Securities and Exchange Commission (SEC) registration). As a result, non-US companies seeking low cost debt have to issue single premium put convertibles in the Euromarket instead.

Chapter 4

❖

Convertible versus bond with equity warrants issue

The question is often asked whether a convertible or a bond with equity warrants issue makes more sense. The answer is that in most circumstances a convertible is more advantageous because it offers superior valuation for the equity option, a longer term investor base, and greater call flexibility (the ability to force the investor to convert into equity), and these advantages usually outweigh the principal advantage of a bond with warrants issue, namely the ability to currency or interest rate swap the bond portion. Each trade-off between the two types of financing, together with other less important trade-offs relating to differences in maturity, tax and accounting, is reviewed in detail below.

Valuation

As a general rule, the theoretical (Black–Scholes) value of an equity warrant often substantially exceeds its market value. Sometimes investors pay as little as one-half to two-thirds of what the warrant in theory is worth. In contrast, convertibles are often fairly valued by the market; discrepancies are small by comparison to those in the warrant market.

There are some important exceptions to this generalisation. In particular, in very strong bull markets warrants are especially attractive to investors and are much more likely to command fair value; indeed in some particularly strong bull markets the market value of warrants sometimes exceeds their theoretical value. In addition, in the more sophisticated capital markets (the United States, for example) investors are more willing to recognise and pay fair value. However, as a general rule, in most markets and on most occasions, companies are paid more for the equity option in a convertible than for that in a warrant.

Investor base

Warrant investors by their nature are more short-term, often investing in warrants without having a long-term interest in owning the underlying equity. Holding periods are generally short, and there is little if any desire to exercise the warrant into the underlying equity. In contrast, convertible investors can be much longer-term, viewing the convertible as an attractive long-term alternative to investing directly in the underlying equity.

The difference between the two is important for companies wishing to expand their investor base and avoid putting downward pressure on their stock price. Issuing warrants runs the risk that in the long-term the only investors interested in owning the warrants are existing shareholders, who may have to sell part of their shareholdings in order to exercise the warrants, creating downward pressure on the stock price. On the other hand, a properly structured and marketed convertible offering can create new investors with a long-term interest in investing not only in the convertible, but also in the underlying equity.

Call flexibility

Bonds with warrants are usually non-callable: the company has no ability to influence the investor's decision as to when and whether to exercise. This is the opposite to the case with a convertible, where the company usually has considerable flexibility to influence the timing of conversion. This is important for companies viewing a hybrid equity issue as an alternative method of raising permanent equity capital − the convertible offers the company the ability to influence the outcome of whether this becomes the case. In contrast, a bond with warrants issue offers no such flexibility.

Swappability

The bond portion of a bond with warrants issue can be currency or interest rate swapped without risk. In contrast, performing a swap on a convertible runs the risk that the convertible will be converted before the swap matures, leaving an unhedged currency or interest rate exposure on the swap.

This attribute of a bond with warrants offering is often considered more important than all its drawbacks, particularly for companies wishing to issue in a foreign market or currency but unwilling to live with the currency risk. A bond with warrants offering can be swapped back into the home currency, unlike a convertible. For this reason many Japanese companies have issued bonds with warrants offerings in the international markets in recent years, rather than convertibles.

Maturity

The bond portion of a bond with warrants offering will remain outstanding until it matures. In contrast a convertible will remain outstanding only for as long as it is not converted. The timing of this is unpredictable, which gives some companies slightly more problems in financial planning than is the case with a bond with warrants issue. In practice, few convertibles are converted by investors early (because the downside protection afforded by the redemption feature is lost upon conversion), with the result that the problem becomes more manageable in practice than theory might suggest.

Tax

Only the coupon (or in some cases, yield to put or maturity) on a convertible is deductible for tax purposes; in contrast, the true interest cost of the bond portion of a bond with warrants offering is usually tax deductible. Since the true interest cost is usually higher than the coupon (or yield to put), tax deductions available on a bond with warrants issue are usually greater than those on a convertible. In most cases, however, the extra tax deductions from a bond with warrants issue are not material, and are not usually considered sufficient to offset its principal drawbacks.

Accounting

A convertible is more advantageous in terms of reported earnings: only the coupon (or yield to put) is recorded as interest expense, and this is usually lower than the interest expense of a bond with warrants offering (i.e. the true yield on the bond portion). On the other hand, a bond with warrants issue can be more advantageous in terms of reported earnings per share, in that in some countries (the United States for example) fully diluted earnings per share is unaffected until the warrants are in the money, whereas on a convertible, fully diluted earnings per share always reflects the extra shares potentially being issued regardless of whether the convertible is in or out of the money. In addition, a bond with warrants issue is more advantageous in terms of balance sheet impact: the warrant portion can be credited immediately to shareholders' equity; in contrast convertible debt remains debt until converted. Again, these are minor differences which are not usually material.

Chapter 5

❖

Summary and conclusions

A convertible financing is usually more advantageous than a bond with warrants offering, and can be more advantageous than an issue of straight debt or straight equity. A conventional or rolling premium put convertible is likely to be converted and will sell shares at a higher price than a straight issue of equity. A single premium put or zero coupon convertible has a much greater probability of being redeemed, and will raise debt at significant savings relative to straight debt rates. A rolling premium put convertible offers a higher effective conversion price than a conventional convertible, but at the cost of a lower probability of conversion. A zero coupon convertible offers similar or greater savings on straight debt rates than a single premium put convertible, and is less likely to be converted, but its use is restricted primarily to the US domestic market.

Part III

❖

The investor's perspective

Chapter 6

❖

The rationale for investing in convertibles

For the traditional investor with a typical investment portfolio comprised of bonds, stocks and cash, there are at least four interrelated reasons why investing in convertibles can make sense:

1. Convertibles offer the best attributes of stocks and bonds, combining the long-run growth potential of stocks with the safety and income advantages of bonds.
2. In efficient markets, most convertibles offer a more attractive risk-adjusted return than their underlying stocks. In addition, in rising stock markets, convertibles will outperform their equivalent straight bonds.
3. The markets are not efficient, with the result that there are many occasions when the convertible's theoretical advantages are even more pronounced in practice.
4. Convertibles now comprise a significant part of most developed countries' financial assets, and no investment portfolio is complete without at least some exposure to them.

For the specialist portfolio manager, managing a portfolio of either bonds or stocks, adding convertibles can also make sense:

1. For the stock portfolio manager most types of convertible in most kinds of market should outperform an equivalent portfolio of cash and shares, i.e. the downside risks will be similar, but the expected returns from the convertible will be higher. As a result, it can be advantageous to replace some of the shares and cash in the stock portfolio with an equivalent investment in convertibles.

2. For stock portfolio managers who are considering convertibles as an alternative to shares only (i.e. excluding cash), adding convertibles will reduce overall expected returns, but reduce risks still further. On a risk adjusted basis, the convertible portfolio's return will be superior even if, in absolute terms, it is lower.
3. For the bond portfolio manager all convertibles will outperform bonds in a strong stock market. The reduction in yield which results from switching into convertibles will be more than offset by an increase in the convertibles' capital value. As a result, in a bull stock market, it can be advantageous to replace some of the bonds in the bond portfolio with an equivalent investment in convertibles.

A 'health warning' is appropriate here. Not all convertibles will behave as expected. There are several drawbacks and pitfalls to convertible investing. In particular, convertibles are complex securities whose price behaviour requires more time and effort to understand than straight bonds and stocks. In addition, convertible portfolios need to be more actively monitored and traded than stock or bond portfolios. Furthermore, an unexpected rise in interest rates, or a takeover bid, or a decline in secondary market liquidity, can all lead to underperformance of convertibles relative to bonds or stocks. Provided, however, that all these risks are fully taken into account, adding convertibles to a typical bond or stock portfolio can enhance portfolio performance.

Convertibles combine the best of bonds and stocks

The traditional investor purchases bonds because they offer preservation of capital and a high, fixed return over a fixed time period for limited downside risk. Equally, stocks are purchased because they offer a high potential return over the long term, albeit with greater near term downside risks.

In a sense, convertibles combine the best of both worlds. The bond component of a convertible ensures that capital is preserved, and offers a reasonably high fixed return over a fixed time period in return for relatively low downside risk, while the conversion option ensures that if the underlying stock does appreciate, the convertible investor will not miss out. In the risk/reward spectrum of investment alternatives, convertibles fit neatly between bonds and stocks, as follows:

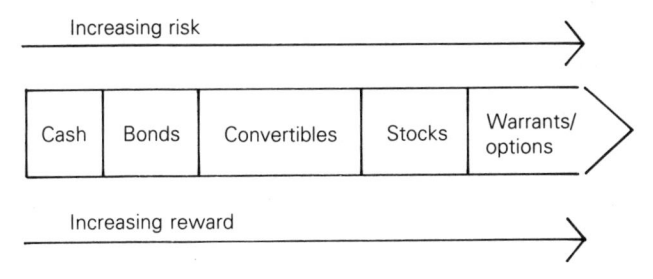

```
          Increasing risk →
    ┌─────┬───────┬─────────────┬────────┬──────────┐
    │ Cash│ Bonds │ Convertibles│ Stocks │ Warrants/│
    │     │       │             │        │ options  │
    └─────┴───────┴─────────────┴────────┴──────────┘
          Increasing reward →
```

The combination of the long-run growth potential of stocks, together with the income, capital preservation and safety advantages of bonds, makes convertibles an attractive alternative for the cautious investor. Although the expected return from a convertible will not be as high as that of straight stocks, nor the risks as low as those of straight bonds, convertibles are an ideal compromise between the two, combining the most attractive features of each security into one package. For this reason, convertibles are particularly attractive to financial trustees, investment advisors, and other fiduciaries charged with the responsibility of managing money in which preservation of capital is essential, but where ideally over the long-term capital appreciation is also strongly desired.

Convertibles offer superior performance over bonds and stocks

Even in an efficient market, most convertibles can offer superior returns, on a risk-adjusted basis, than their underlying stocks. At the same time, in rising stock markets, convertibles will outperform their equivalent straight bonds. The first statement is easiest to understand for conventional high coupon convertibles. Although the convertible costs more than its underlying stock (the difference in cost being the conversion premium), it offers greater benefits which over time tend to offset the additional cost. The convertible's coupon usually exceeds the dividend on the stock and, in addition, the convertible offers the possibility of principal repayment at final maturity. At some point in the future, at the end of what is termed the convertible's breakeven or payback period, the convertible's extra income will have offset its extra cost, so that the convertible's remaining benefits become free from this point onwards. Since in every other respect the convertible offers what the stock offers, the convertible is the superior investment alternative.

For low coupon convertibles or convertibles with long payback or breakeven periods, the first statement is less obvious and requires more careful explanation. It is reviewed in more detail below, and a large part of the next chapter is devoted to examining it in even greater detail. At this stage, it is probably sufficient to mention that as a general rule, a convertible offers two-thirds of the upside reward potential of the underlying equity, in return for just one-third of the downside risk. Although in absolute terms the convertible's expected return is lower, once risk is taken into account its performance is superior.

The attractions of convertibles to bond investors are easier to understand. In strong stock markets, such as those which prevailed before the October 1987 crash, it makes sense to replace bond portfolios with convertibles because convertibles will outperform straight bonds: the appreciation in the convertible's capital value will more than offset the loss in yield. The best way of illustrating the attractions of convertibles to both bond and stock investors is to consider a specific example. Suppose ABC Company issues a fifteen year convertible with a 7% coupon and a 20% conversion premium, which becomes callable after three years. ABC's shares trade at $50 each, and pay an annual dividend of $2 to yield 4%. ABC's long-term (fifteen year) straight bonds yield 10½%.

For the stock investor, an investment in the convertible costs 20% more than a direct investment in the same number of underlying shares, the difference in cost being the conversion premium on the convertible. In return for this, the convertible yields a greater income than the stock (7% coupon versus 4% dividend) and also offers the potential of repayment of principal in fifteen years' time if not converted beforehand. The best way of determining whether it makes sense for the stock investor to invest in the convertible instead of the stock is to estimate the likely range of returns from the convertible and compare them with the corresponding returns from holding the stock. Suppose that ABC's business prospects, and the stock market's prospects, are such that it is reasonable to expect that ABC's share price over the next year is likely to be within 25% of its current level (i.e. in the range of $37½ to $62½) with the most likely range within 10% (i.e. $45 to $55). The range of potential returns (including dividend income) at the end of the year from an investment in the stock would then be as follows:

Stock price	Stock return
$37½	−21%
$45	− 6%
$50	+ 4%
$55	+14%
$62½	+29%

Investing in the stock would yield a return ranging from −21% to +29%, with the most probable range from −6% to +14%. (In this and all future examples, tax considerations will be ignored in order to facilitate the calculations).

In order to determine the equivalent range of returns for the convertible, it is first necessary to estimate the market value of the convertible for each possible future stock price. This is the hardest part, particularly for those without access to a computer valuation model. For the most accurate results, a computer valuation model is best; in the absence of this, however, one of the manual techniques described in Part IV can be used. Either method should yield the following results:

Stock price	Estimated convertible price
$37½	87%
$45	94%
$50	99%
$55	105%
$62½	114%

Thus, for example, if ABC's share price fell to $37½, the convertible would fall to 87% of par. Correspondingly, if ABC's share price increased to $62½, the convertible would be worth 114% of par. When coupon income of 7% is taken into account, the range of returns for the convertible is as follows:

Stock price	Estimated convertible price	Resulting convertible return
$37½	87%	− 6%
$45	94%	+ 1%
$50	99%	+ 6%
$55	105%	+12%
$62½	114%	+21%

When compared side by side, the superior performance characteristics of the convertible begin to emerge:

Stock price	Stock return	Convertible return
$37½	−21%	− 6%
$45	− 6%	+ 1%
$50	+ 4%	+ 6%
$55	+14%	+12%
$62½	+29%	+21%

Over the range of possible future share prices, investing in the convertible will yield almost two-thirds of the upside reward of investing in the stock (21% versus 29%) for just under one-third of the downside risk (−6% versus −21%). Over the most likely range, the convertible will yield almost all of the upside in the stock (12% versus 14%) for almost negligible downside (+1% versus −6%). On this basis, the convertible's performance is superior, even if in absolute terms, the best case is not as rewarding as that of the stock.

For the bond investor, the convertible will outperform an investment in the equivalent straight bond only if its total return exceeds the return on straight bonds of 10½%. This would occur when the convertible's market value at the end of the year was above 103½%. This will happen if the stock price is approximately $53½, or 7% more than its value at the beginning of the year. If the stock rises by more than 7%, the convertible will outperform the equivalent straight bond; similarly if the stock rises by less than 7%, the convertible will underperform. This demonstrates that the convertible makes sense for the bond investor, but only in a rising stock market. Lengthening the investment horizon reinforces the case for the convertible. For example, on a five year horizon, suppose the most probable range of stock prices is $25 to $100, i.e. minus 50% to plus 100% relative to its current level. (The asymmetry between the best and worst cases is deliberate: stock prices are usually expected to appreciate in the long run, even if in the short run there are fluctuations either way.) The range of possible returns would then be as follows:

THE RATIONALE FOR INVESTING IN CONVERTIBLES

Stock price	Per annum stock return	Estimated convertible price	Per annum convertible return
$25	− 8%	82%	+4%
$37½	− 1%	88%	+5%
$50	+ 4%	96%	+6%
$62½	+ 8%	104%	+8%
$75	+12%	125%	+11%
$100	+18%	167%	+17%

Note: Assumes dividends change in line with stock price, i.e. dividend yield is unchanged.

Over the likely range of future share prices, the convertible enjoys nearly all the upside potential of the stock (+17% p.a. versus +18% p.a.) for negligible downside risk (+4% p.a. versus −8% p.a.). Similarly the bond investor will be better off owning the convertible, but only in a strong stock market. The convertible's performance is superior only if its return exceeds 10½% per annum over the next five years. A simple calculation shows that this would occur if the convertible appreciated to 121½% at the end of the fifth year, which, in turn, would happen if the stock rose to approximately $73, a rise of 46% over five years.

While this example is hypothetical, the results are representative, in general, of the performance potential of most convertibles. Barring an unforeseen rise in interest rates, or a corporate takeover, or a decline in secondary market liquidity, (the major risks in convertible investing), most convertibles offer the stock investor much of the upside potential in stock investing in return for significantly reduced downside risk, and the bond investor superior performance in bull stock markets. The stock investor can reflect the superior performance potential of convertibles by replacing some of the shares held in the investment portfolio, together with some cash, with an equivalent investment in convertibles. Provided the proportion of cash to stock is chosen correctly, the convertible portfolio will have the same downward risks as the combined stock/cash portfolio, but higher upside rewards.

The convertible markets are inefficient

The efficient market theoretical advantages of convertibles outlined above can be even more attractive in practice because the convertible markets are far from perfect. Perhaps because of their complexity, the convertible markets are not efficient, and there are often some very attractive investment opportunities which can turn a marginal theoretical advantage into an extemely attractive practical one. For example, Eurosterling convertibles issued by UK companies have for some time been relatively inexpensive. For investors in the underlying equity (for example UK domestic equity investors), the equivalent Euroconvertible often offers a substantial increase in yield and downside protection relative to the underlying shares, in return for a negligible premium in cost. The rewards of swapping out of the shares into the convertible (namely yield pick-up and increase in downside protection) are currently much greater, and the costs (namely premium) much lower than they have been for some time, with the result that some of the Euroconvertibles are a veritable bargain.

Example

In 1987 Tesco, the major UK stores group, issued a £115 million Euroconvertible, details of which are as follows:

Issue amount:	£115 million
Maturity date:	20 February 2002
Coupon:	4% payable annually on 20 February
Investor put option:	At 127.625%, on 20 February 1992
Issuer call options:	Only if share price exceeds 130% of conversion price
Conversion dates:	Continuous – conversion permitted at any time
Conversion price:	£1.74
Recent share price:	£1.88
Recent bond price:	110%
Parity value:	108%
Stock yield:	2.5%

For an investor owning the shares of Tesco, a switch into the bonds would cost 2% in premium (the difference between the convertible's market price and its parity value), in return for which the investor would benefit from a 1.5% increase in yield (the difference between the convertible's coupon and the stock's yield) and the certainty of almost 18% appreciation in the capital value of the portfolio, obtained by exercising the put option in February 1992. The extra cost of the convertible relative to the shares would be recouped in just over a year; from this point onwards the convertible investor would be in the same position as the stock investor, except for the additional benefits of the yield pick-up and guaranteed capital appreciation.

Of course, situations like this do not persist and over time this particular opportunity will disappear as more UK equity investors discover the attractions of UK Euroconvertibles and swap into them from the underlying equity. The good news is that this process usually takes some time, and in the meantime other opportunities are likely to appear.

The world's major convertible markets are significant

Over the last few years, convertibles have become a major component of the world's financial system. In Japan, for example, companies raise more money from convertible issues than they do from any other type of security. While the amount raised by Western companies from convertibles is a lower percentage of the total, it is still significant:

1988 New Issue Volume [1]

	Japanese companies [2] Volume	%	US companies Volume	%
Bonds	$ 10bn	7%	$140bn	78%
Convertibles	60bn	43	5bn	3
Bonds with warrants	35bn	25	negligible	—
Stocks	35bn	25	35bn	19
	$140bn	100%	$180bn	100%

Notes: [1] Total funds raised in both domestic and overseas markets.
[2] Fiscal year 1988

The pattern in most Western countries is similar to that of the United States, where almost 15–20% of all forms of equity and equity-linked fund raising (including common stock and preferred share issues) is done in the form of convertibles. Because convertibles form such a significant part of the corporate sector's fund raising activity, no major investment portfolio is complete without at least some exposure to them.

Common misconceptions about convertibles

There are several misconceptions about the merits of convertibles which are often held up as reasons for not investing.

Because some of them are fairly common, many readers are likely to be conscious of them, so it probably makes sense to address them here in order not to detract from what follows. One common misconception often put forward is that it is not necessary to invest directly in convertibles because it is possible to create a synthetic convertible by investing in a combination of other, less complex, securities, such as bonds, shares and options or warrants. A second misconception is that it only makes sense to invest in convertibles when the underlying equity is expected to appreciate, but that if this were the case, then a direct investment in the shares themselves would be preferable, because they would be more rewarding. If it were not the case, then higher yielding straight bonds would be more rewarding. Either way, there is an investment alternative which is superior to the convertible.

Both views are misleading. Firstly, it is not possible to create a synthetic convertible by investing in a combination of other securities. A convertible offers a unique set of risks and rewards which cannot be duplicated elsewhere. For example, a combination of bonds and stocks fails to reflect the option component embedded in a convertible. Equally, a combination of bonds with warrants or options (although similar in many other respects) fails to reflect the uniqueness of the conversion option in a convertible. A convertible can be converted only by tendering the bond. In contrast, warrants and options can be exercised only with cash. In a package of bonds with warrants, it may or may not be possible to exercise the warrants from the proceeds of selling the bonds, depending on the prevailing level of interest rates. If interest rates are high, selling the bonds may raise an amount which is insufficient to exercise the warrants, and vice versa. Investing in a convertible incurs no such interest rate risk.

Secondly, while it is true to say that it makes sense to invest in convertibles only when the underlying equity is expected to appreciate, it does not necessarily mean that the equity should be preferred instead. Investing in the underlying equity certainly offers greater rewards, but it also carries greater risks, and account should be taken of this. In fact, as has been mentioned previously, most convertibles offer returns which on a risk-adjusted basis are superior to those of the underlying equity, even if in absolute terms they are lower.

Put another way, the argument that it makes sense to prefer equities over convertibles can be extended further to suggest that it makes sense to ignore equities completely and invest only in warrants and options. The same logic applies: warrants and options offer even higher prospective returns than either equities or convertibles, so that if it made sense to purchase equities, it would make even more sense to purchase warrants and options instead. This is fallacious, as every rational investor knows, because of the considerably greater risks involved in warrant and option investing. Convertibles offer a blend of risks and rewards which, although lower than those of equities and warrants or options, are sufficiently attractive in their own right so that in many cases the convertible is the superior investment alternative. Notwithstanding this, there are some legitimate drawbacks to convertible investing. Not all convertibles offer superior risk-adjusted returns: in particular, there are some types of convertibles (e.g. many zero coupon convertibles) that offer inferior risk-adjusted returns. In addition, an unexpected rise in interest rates, or a takeover bid, or a dramatic collapse in secondary market liquidity such as occurred in many convertibles in the October 1987 crash, can also lead to underperformance. Every convertible and every situation is unique, and careful analysis, using some of the methodology outlined here, is appropriate before determining whether the generalisations presented here are true to the specific situation.

Methods of approaching convertible investing

There are at least five basic guidelines which, if followed, will help the discerning investor to determine whether adding convertibles to an investment portfolio makes sense.

1. Investigate whether the underlying equity is a worthwhile purchase. If the underlying shares are not recommended for purchase, then it is unlikely that the convertible will make sense.
2. Assess whether the convertible offers a more attractive set of risks and rewards than the underlying shares, using some of the techniques outlined here.
3. Give careful consideration to the extent to which some of the risks of convertible investing outlined later might apply.
4. For any existing shares held in the investment portfolio, investigate whether there is a convertible alternative. Very few brokers regularly mention convertibles as an alternative to shares, yet for the reasons outlined above, convertibles can be more attractive than the underlying equity.

5. In strong stock markets (and only in strong stock markets), consider replacing some of the bonds in the portfolio with their equivalent convertibles.

The first guideline is the most important. The rigorous investor will perform an analysis of the company's business and prospects before investing in the convertible. In almost every case, only if the equity is attractive for purchase does it make sense to consider the convertible: companies with indifferent or poor earnings prospects are likely to have indifferent or poor performing convertibles. Movements in the company's share price are usually the single most important influence on the price of a convertible. The second and third guidelines are also important and the subject of much of the next two chapters. The fourth guideline is often overlooked. Few equity investors and few equity brokers are actively conscious of convertible alternatives, despite the fact that these may be more attractive. For the discerning investor, switching out of equities into convertibles (and when the time is right, back again into equities) can be very rewarding. The last guideline applies only in bull stock markets and requires little by the way of additional explanation.

Chapter 7

❖

Types of convertible

The purpose of this chapter is to describe the different types of convertible that can be invested in, and to provide a framework for assessing whether the convertible is a more attractive investment than its equivalent stock or bond. From the investor's perspective, there are essentially four types of convertible available for investment:

1. Low premium convertibles
2. Conventional convertibles
3. Premium put convertibles
4. Zero coupon convertibles

Almost all convertibles issued by companies in the world's major convertible markets fall into one of the categories above. They are usually issued in one of two forms: either as convertible bonds (debt) or as convertible preferred (equity), although convertible preferred is much less common than convertible debt. Each type of convertible has a different set of risk/reward characteristics: for example low premium convertibles offer a much greater proportion of the rewards of investing in the stock than do zero coupon convertibles; equally their downside risks are larger. This is illustrated overleaf, continuing with the hypothetical example of ABC Company discussed in the previous chapter.

Low premium convertibles

Convertibles in this category include all convertibles which are originally offered with a very low conversion premium (around 5%). Low premium convertibles generally also have low coupons to match. Almost all convertibles issued by Japanese companies are low premium convertibles, regardless of where they are issued (principally Japan, the Euromarket and Swiss market). Issuance by Western companies is rare, although there are some sporadic examples. Since Japanese companies issue more convertibles than anyone else, low premium convertibles are the most common type of convertible available for investment. Some Japanese low premium convertibles, particularly those issued in the international markets, are offered with early redemption rights for the investor (put options). The put option changes the risk characteristics of these securities fairly significantly, with the result that they more properly fall into the category of premium put convertible discussed later. In our hypothetical example for ABC, were ABC to issue a low premium convertible in the Euromarket, the terms would be as follows:

Maturity	Fifteen years
Coupon	5%
Conversion premium	5%
Call options	Non-callable for three years
Put options	None

On a one year investment horizon, using either a computer-based valuation package or one of the manual valuation techniques described in Part IV, the expected value of the convertible and the corresponding investment returns would be as follows:

Stock price	Stock return	Estimated convertible price	Convertible return
$37½	−21%	83%	−12%
$45	− 6%	93%	− 2%
$50	+ 4%	100%	+ 5%
$55	+14%	108%	+13%
$62½	+29%	120%	+25%

It can be seen that the convertible offers almost 85% of the upside reward of the stock (+25% versus +29%), but only 60% of the downside risk (−12% versus −21%). On a risk-adjusted basis, the convertible's expected performance is superior. The convertible will outperform the equivalent straight bond if its return exceeds 10½%. This occurs only if its value at the end of the year exceeds 105½%. For this to happen, the stock price would need to rise to $53, equivalent to a 6% rate of appreciation over the year, again illustrating the point that a convertible makes sense as an alternative to straight bonds in rising stock markets only.

Conventional convertibles

These include all convertibles with a traditional conversion premium, i.e. one which is around 20%, but which can vary from as little as 10% to as much as 30%. Conventional convertibles also carry higher coupons to compensate the investor for the extra premium, and do not offer any put options for the investor. (Those that do more properly fall into the category of premium put convertible described later.) Nearly all convertibles issued in the domestic markets in the major Western countries (principally the United States, United Kingdom and France) fall into this category. Many Euroconvertibles also fall into this category, as does the convertible analysed in the last chapter for ABC. As a reminder, the terms for ABC's convertible were:

Maturity	Fifteen years
Coupon	7%
Conversion premium	20%
Call options	Non-callable for three years
Put options	None

The convertible's anticipated investment performance was as follows:

Stock price	Stock return	Estimated convertible price	Convertible return
$37½	−21%	87%	− 6%
$45	− 6%	94%	− 1%
$50	+ 4%	99%	+ 6%
$55	+14%	105%	+12%
$62½	+29%	114%	+21%

For the stock investor, the conventional convertible offers two-thirds of the upside reward potential in the stock for only one-third of the downside risk. As a result of this, it is less rewarding (and less risky) than the low premium convertible. For the bond investor the conventional convertible will outperform the straight bond equivalent only if the underlying stock appreciates by more than 7%.

Premium put convertibles

Premium put convertibles include all convertibles where the investor has a right to redeem the bonds early, usually at a significant premium to their issue price (hence the term premium put), but sometimes at the issue price itself. The conversion premium can be as low as that of low premium convertibles (Japanese premium put convertibles fall into this category), or as high or slightly higher than that on conventional convertibles (as is the case for most premium put convertibles issued by Western companies). The compensation for the issuer (and the cost to the investor) in offering the early redemption right comes in the form of the coupon, which is usually lower than that on other types of convertible.

In some premium put convertibles, particularly those offered in the Euromarket, the investor's put option is repeated to create a so-called 'rolling' or 'flexible' put. Such repetition usually makes no difference to the convertible's risk/reward characteristics, because the issuer also retains the right to call the bonds on the first put date at the put price. Premium put convertibles are almost exclusively the preserve of the Swiss market and the Euromarket. Issues have been made by a wide variety of Japanese and Western companies, including borrowers from the United States, United Kingdom, Australia and continental Europe. In some respects, the premium put convertible is the most popular type of convertible in the Euromarkets with both issuers and investors alike. Typical terms for an issue by ABC in the Euromarkets would be as follows:

Maturity	Fifteen years
Coupon	4%
Conversion premium	20%
Call options	Callable at any time at a small declining premium to par, but in the first five years, only if the share price is 130% of the initial conversion price
Put options	Puttable at 123½% (to yield 8%) at the end of the fifth year

The expected range of returns from the premium put over a one year time horizon are as follows:

Stock price	Stock return	Estimated convertible price	Convertible return
$37½	−21%	96%	0%
$45	− 6%	100%	+ 4%
$50	+ 4%	103%	+ 7%
$55	+14%	107%	+11%
$62½	+29%	114%	+18%

In this example, the premium put convertible offers the stock investor more than 60% of the upside reward in the stock (18% versus 29%), in return for negligible downside risk (0% versus -21%). In this respect the premium put is less risky and rewarding than either the conventional or low coupon convertibles. A similar calculation also shows that the bond investor benefits from investing in a premium put convertible, but only if the stock appreciates 9%.

Zero coupon convertibles

A zero coupon convertible is just what it says: a convertible without a coupon. Most zero coupon convertibles to date have been issued either in the US domestic market, where they are more popularly referred to as LYONs (short for Liquid Yield Option Notes), or by Japanese companies in the Swiss market. LYONs typically are issued at a substantial discount to their face value, and are puttable at various points during their life, usually starting after three to five years. The put prices are at steadily increasing levels to provide the investor with a constant yield between puts equal to the original yield to maturity of the bonds. On some LYONs the puts are for cash ('hard put'); on others, the put is satisfied by the issue of other securities with a market value equivalent to the put price ('soft put'). The initial conversion premium at around 15% is usually lower than that found on a conventional convertible from the same borrower.

Japanese zero coupon convertibles in the Swiss market offer an even lower conversion premium, around 5%, and are usually structured as a zero coupon premium put convertible, i.e. offered at par and redeemable at a premium, rather than as a discount priced bond. Typical terms for a LYONs type zero coupon convertible issue by ABC are as follows:

Maturity	Fifteen years
Coupon	Zero
Conversion premium	15%
Issue price	34% to yield 7½% to maturity
Call options	Non-callable for three years. Callable thereafter at accreted value provided share price is a specified percentage of initial conversion price
Put options	Puttable at 48½% after five years to yield 7½%, and periodically thereafter

The expected range of returns is as follows:

Stock price	Stock return	Estimated convertible price	Convertible return
$37½	−21%	33%	− 3%
$45	− 6%	34%	0%
$50	+ 4%	35½%	+ 4%
$55	+14%	37%	+ 9%
$62½	+29%	39½%	+16%

At first sight, this seems to repeat the previous pattern: the convertible enjoys a proportion of the stock's upside for little of the downside risk. However, and very much in contrast to the other types of convertible, this type of convertible is not attractive to stock investors, because the stock investor can create a portfolio with exactly the same downside risk, but with higher upside rewards, by investing partly in the stock and partly in cash or cash equivalents (e.g. Treasury bills or bonds). For example, if a one year investment in Treasury bills yields 8%, and the investor invests 38% of the portfolio in stock and 62% in cash, the combined stock/cash portfolio would produce the following range of returns:

Stock price	38:62 stock:cash portfolio return	Convertible return
$37½	− 3%	− 3%
$45	+ 3%	0%
$50	+ 6%	+ 4%
$55	+10%	+ 9%
$62½	+16%	+16%

The combination stock/cash portfolio has an identical 'best' and 'worst' case to that of the convertible, but a more attractive performance in all other cases. In most cases, therefore, the stock investor will be better off with a stock/cash portfolio than with the convertible. The bond investor, on the other hand, continues to benefit from owning the convertible, but in this case only if the stock price appreciates by more than 6%.

Adjusting for risk

The analysis of the zero coupon convertible showed that once the stock investor had compensated for the extra risks in stock investing by keeping a proportion of the stock portfolio invested in cash, the blended cash/stock portfolio offered similar downside risk to that of the convertible, but better returns in all other cases (except the best). In other words, after adjusting for the different risks, and putting both securities on an equal footing, the convertible underperformed the underlying stock. The discerning investor might ask whether this was the case for the other types of convertible, since, up until now, all that has been demonstrated is that convertibles offer a proportion of the upside rewards in return for a lower proportion of the downside risks. This part of the chapter shows that even after adjusting for risk, most convertibles (except zero coupon convertibles) continue to offer superior investment performance over the underlying stock. A little algebra shows that if R_c is the expected return on the convertible, R_s that of stock, and d that of cash, then the risks of stock investing can be reduced to that of convertible investing by keeping a proportion of the stock portfolio invested in cash according to the following formula:

$$\text{Cash percentage} = \frac{R_s - R_c}{R_s - d}$$

This formula can now be applied to each type of convertible in turn to show that in almost every case, on a risk-adjusted basis, the convertible's expected returns are superior to those of the underlying stock.

Conventional convertible

The example for ABC at the beginning of this chapter showed that the worst case expected return from owning ABC's convertible was −6%. By comparison the worst case expected return from owning ABC's stock was −21%. If one year Treasury bills can be purchased to yield 8%, then the worst case risks of owning ABC's stock can be reduced to that of the convertible by investing the following percentage of the stock portfolio in cash:

$$\frac{(-21)-(-6)}{(-21)-(8)} = 52\%$$

A portfolio which is 52% invested in cash or Treasury bills and 48% in stock would then produce a profile of returns as follows:

Stock price	Stock return	Conventional convertible return	Stock/cash portfolio return
$37½	−21%	− 6%	− 6%
$45	− 6%	+ 1%	+ 1%
$50	+ 4%	+ 6%	+ 6%
$55	+14%	+12%	+11%
$62½	+29%	+21%	+18%

It can be seen that the combination portfolio has a broadly similar pattern of returns to the convertible, except in the best cases, where the convertible outperforms. On a risk-adjusted basis, the convertible's performance is the more attractive. In fact, the more the stock appreciates, the more the convertible will outperform. Given that in purchasing the stock in the first place, the investor's expectation is that it will appreciate, the investor wishing to participate in the upside of the stock but hedge some of the downside risk would be better off owning the convertible than the underlying stock.

Low premium convertible

The worst case expected return from owning ABC's low premium convertible was −12%. Running the formula above, the

TYPES OF CONVERTIBLE

proportion of the stock/cash portfolio to be invested in cash would be 31%. The combination portfolio would yield the following range of returns:

Stock price	Stock return	Convertible return	Combination portfolio return
$37½	−21%	−12%	−12%
$45	− 6%	− 2%	− 2%
$50	+ 4%	+ 5%	+ 5%
$55	+14%	+13%	+12%
$62½	+29%	+25%	+22%

The combination portfolio has similar downside risks to the convertible, but underperforms on the upside so that the convertible is again superior to the stock on a risk-adjusted basis.

Premium put convertible

The worst case expected return from owning ABC's convertible was 0%. As a consequence, using the formula above, the proportion of cash in the combination stock/cash portfolio would be 72%. The combination portfolio would yield the following range of returns:

Stock price	Stock return	Convertible return	Combination portfolio return
$37½	−21%	0%	0%
$45	− 6%	+ 4%	+ 4%
$50	+ 4%	+ 7%	+ 7%
$55	+14%	+11%	+10%
$62½	+29%	+18%	+14%

As can be seen, the premium put convertible is also superior to the combination portfolio, although the premium put's advantage is more marked than in the other cases.

This analysis shows that in all except the zero coupon case, the stock investor will produce generally higher returns, on a risk adjusted basis, by investing in the convertible rather than the underlying stock.

Chapter 8

❖

Pitfalls in convertible investing

So far this part of the book has dwelt mainly on the rewards of convertible investing, focusing only in a limited fashion on the pitfalls and drawbacks. There are several of these which need to be carefully evaluated before any decisions are taken to invest in convertibles. The principal pitfalls which can lead to a convertible underperforming its underlying stock and bond include the following:

1. A major rise in long-term interest rates.
2. A takeover.
3. A decline in secondary market trading liquidity.
4. The company entering a period of business and financial difficulty.

The principal drawbacks of convertible investing relative to stock or bond investing include:

1. The need to trade convertible portfolios more actively. For example, outperformance of conventional convertibles applies only to par-priced securities: convertibles trading substantially above or below par offer different risk/reward characteristics with fewer advantages over the underlying stock or bond.
2. The need to monitor convertible portfolios more actively for, e.g., call notices and significant price movements necessitating a trading decision.
3. The very complexity of convertibles. Any reader of this book will appreciate that convertibles are more complex securities than bonds or stocks, and require greater time and effort to evaluate and fully understand.

PITFALLS IN CONVERTIBLE INVESTING

Each of these is described in more detail below.

Interest rates

A major rise in interest rates can eliminate the advantages of a convertible to a stock investor (although not necessarily to a bond investor). One of the principal reasons why the convertible outperforms its underlying stock is that its value holds up when the stock declines, but rises when the stock rises. The main reason why its value holds up when stock prices decline is that a floor on the convertible's value is provided by its bond value. Even though the share price may fall, the convertible will never trade below its bond value. If long-term interest rates rise, the convertible's bond value will decline. As a consequence, the convertible's market value may decline in periods of rising interest rates as quickly as the underlying stock price, with the result that the convertible offers no advantage over the underlying stock. This is illustrated below, using the conventional convertible for ABC as an example. Two scenarios are analysed: one where it is assumed that there is no change in interest rates, and another where interest rates are assumed to rise 3% over the year (i.e. a fairly substantial rise):

		No change in interest rates		3% increase in interest rates	
Stock price	Stock return	Convertible price	Convertible return	Convertible price	Convertible return
$37½	−21%	87%	−6%	80%	−13%
$45	−6%	94%	+1%	88%	−5%
$50	−4%	99%	+6%	95%	+2%
$55	+14%	105%	+12%	100%	+7%
$62½	+29%	114%	+21%	110%	+17%

A 3% rise in long-term interest rates over the year causes the convertible's market value to decline considerably. Its worst case return (-13%) bears approximately the same ratio to the stock's worst case return (-21%) as its best case return (+17%) does to the stock's best case (+29%). In other words, the convertible has the same ratio of risk and reward as the stock, and offers the stock investor no material advantage. As a consequence, if interest rates are expected to rise substantially, the convertible should be avoided.

Of course the opposite is also true: interest rates can work to the convertible investor's advantage. A significant decline in interest rates over the holding period will increase the convertible's advantage over the stock.

For bond investors, a rise in interest rates does not necessarily eliminate the attractions of the convertible. Although the expected returns from the convertible are reduced, the returns from investing in straight bonds are also reduced and the convertible may still outperform the straight bond if the underlying stock has appreciated in the meantime. For example, an investment in five year bonds yielding 10½% will produce a return of just under 2% at the end of the year if interest rates rise 3%, calculated as follows:

Market value of four year bond with
10½% coupon and 13½% interest rates = 91.2%
Overall return = Market value of bond + coupon paid - original cost
= 91.2 + 10.5 - 100
= 1.7%

As can be seen from the earlier table, an investment in a conventional convertible will produce a return in excess of 2%, even if interest rates rise by 3%, provided the stock price is unchanged or higher at the end of the year. For the bond investor, therefore, the convertible outperforms straight bonds in a falling bond market, provided the share price is unchanged or appreciating. The other side of the coin is also true: a bull market in bonds caused by a fall in interest rates does not eliminate the convertible's attractions to the bond investor, provided the underlying share price is also appreciating. While the straight bond investment will perform particularly well in a declining interest rate environment, the convertible will also outperform if the stock price rises sufficiently.

Takeover

A takeover bid can eliminate the advantages of a convertible to a stock investor, although not necessarily to a bond investor. In all the analysis of convertible investment returns performed so far, the estimated market value of the convertible at the end of the investment horizon has always exceeded its parity value (i.e. the market value of the underlying equity) by an amount equal to its effective conversion premium. This premium is effectively the value to the investor of owning a call option on the shares underlying the convertible with a time value equal to the remaining life of the convertible. If a takeover bid is announced and is successful, the underlying shares will disappear and the remaining life of the convertible can shrink to zero. The call option becomes worthless, and the conversion premium will therefore be eliminated. The convertible's market value will drop to whichever is the higher of its bond value or its parity value. Although the convertible investor may have done well as a result of the takeover (particularly if a significant premium for the underlying stock was paid by the acquiror), it is possible that a direct investment in the underlying stock will have produced much higher returns, not only in absolute terms, but also perhaps more importantly, on a risk adjusted basis as well. The straight bond investor is, of course, largely unaffected by such considerations and may well benefit significantly from owning the convertible if there is a takeover.

Secondary market liquidity

In order to be able to realise investment returns from any portfolio, whether shares, bonds or convertibles, there has to be an active and liquid secondary market. All the analyses performed for convertibles so far have assumed that this is the case, and that the convertibles can be traded at close to their theoretical value. This is not always the case. Convertibles are inherently less liquid than their underlying stocks. Some of the reasons for this include the following:

1. The smaller market capitalisation of convertibles. The market capitalisation of a convertible issue is smaller than the market value of all the company's issued shares, which usually means that the convertible is less liquid. For large blue-chip companies issuing large capitalisation convertibles, the difference in liquidity may not be material, but for smaller companies with small capitalisation convertibles the difference may be significant.
2. Less transparent methods of trading convertibles. Many convertibles are traded over-the-counter by telephone, in contrast to their underlying stocks which can usually be

exchange traded. The price transparency of the over-the-counter market is much lower than that of many stock exchanges.
3. Fewer market makers. The number of market makers in the convertible is usually fewer than that of the underlying stock.
4. Age and price concerns. 'Old' convertibles (i.e. convertibles which have been in issue for some time), or convertibles trading significantly above or below par, are usually less liquid than new issues or issues trading around par, in both cases because of reduced investor interest.

Moreover, in declining stock markets, the liquidity of convertibles can decline more precipitously than the underlying stock. Many investors discovered to their cost that in the stock market crash of October 1987 many convertibles, particularly small capitalisation issues issued by less than blue-chip companies, became impossible to sell. While the events of October 1987 may be considered by many to be extreme, the lessons to be drawn are obvious. A careful assessment of the convertible's future liquidity is essential to determining whether it is likely to outperform its underlying stock.

Business and financial distress

There are many reasons why a company's stock price may decline: one obvious one is that the company's business is not doing so well. If the difficulties are particularly severe and there is a risk of business failure, the bond value of the convertible, which in normal circumstances would hold the convertible's market value up in a period of declining stock prices, may also fall, leading to corresponding falls in the value of the convertible and underperformance of the convertible relative to the stock. In this event, the only advantage that the convertible would offer the stock investor would be priority in repayment in any bankruptcy proceedings. This would need to be carefully weighed against the premium paid over the stock to acquire the convertible in the first place. In most cases, the extra cost may not be worthwhile. This pitfall underlines a point made earlier: that no investment should be made in any convertible until the business and prospects of the company in question have been properly evaluated, and determined to be attractive.

Convertibles trading significantly above or below par

Much more so than stock or bond portfolios, convertible portfolios need to be actively traded if the advantages of convertible investing are to be preserved. As is illustrated below, convertibles trading significantly above or below par value (i.e. redemption value, not parity value) offer fewer benefits to stock and bond investors than do those trading at par. Consequently convertible portfolios have to be continually adjusted so that those standing significantly above or below par are weeded out in favour of par-priced securities.

Above par convertibles

For the stock investor, a convertible trading significantly above par usually offers a pattern of risks and rewards similar to the underlying stock, and is unlikely to prove a more attractive investment. The upside reward is almost identical while the downside risk is only marginally lower, because the convertible's bond value (which would otherwise hold the convertible's market value up in a declining stock price environment) is considerably below its market value. As a consequence, since there is no significant advantage in owning the convertible, it is probable that the stock investor would be better off owning the more liquid underlying stock. This is illustrated using the hypothetical example of the conventional convertible issued by ABC. Suppose after one year ABC's stock price and dividend had doubled to $100 and $4 respectively. The convertible at this point would then be worth approximately 167% of par. Notwithstanding the excellent historic performance, suppose that the most likely range of ABC's future share price over the next year was within 25% of the current price, i.e. in the range $75 to $125. The expected returns from holding the stock and the convertible would then be as follows:

Share price	Stock return	Estimated convertible price	Convertible return
$ 75	−21%	128%	−19%
$ 90	− 6%	150%	− 6%
$100	+ 4%	166%	+ 4%
$110	+14%	183%	+14%
$125	+29%	208%	+29%

The convertible offers a broadly similar profile of risks and rewards, except in the worst case, where it is marginally better. The stock investor would need to evaluate carefully whether this isolated worst case better performance justified the other risks of investing in the convertible (particularly its lower liquidity), or whether it is more advantageous to invest directly in the stock. In most cases, a direct investment in the stock is likely to prove preferable. The bond investor also incurs significant additional risk from purchasing the convertible. While a strong stock price performance may lead to the convertible outperforming the straight bond, the absence of downside protection on the convertible can prove costly.

Below par convertibles

Convertibles standing significantly below par behave more like bonds than stock substitutes, and offer the stock investor little of the rewards of stock investing. Similarly, the bond investor will benefit from owning the convertible only if the share price appreciates by more than that required for a par-priced convertible. Using the example of ABC to illustrate this, suppose that ABC's share price and dividend had dropped at the end of the first year to $25 and $1 respectively. The convertible at this point would be worth 80%. Assume that over the following year, the expected range of future share prices lies between $18¾ and $31¼ (i.e. within 25% of the current price). The expected returns from investing in the stock and the convertible would then be as follows:

Share price	Stock return	Estimated convertible price	Convertible return
$18¾	−21%	78%	+ 6%
$22½	− 6%	79%	+ 7%
$25	+ 4%	80%	+ 9%
$27½	+14%	81%	+10%
$31¼	+29%	83%	+12%

The convertible offers virtually none of the risks and rewards of the stock and is unlikely to make sense as an alternative for the stock investor. Similarly the convertible only outperforms straight bonds yielding 10½% if the share price appreciates by approximately 15% or more, which makes the convertible a less attractive proposition for the bond investor as well.

Need for more active monitoring

Convertible portfolios need to be more actively monitored than their stock or bond counterparts to keep a close look-out for three events in particular:

1. Major price movements in the underlying stock which result in a convertible trading significantly above or below par (redemption) value, so that a trading decision to sell the convertible ought to be made.
2. Significant appreciation in the stock price which permits the issuer to announce early redemption (call) of the convertible. If this occurs, there is usually only a short (thirty day) window for the investor to determine whether to convert or redeem, and there is often no protection for those who fail to heed the call notice and are mandatorily redeemed when the bonds should have been converted.
3. The timing of when the bonds are converted into their underlying stock. On most convertibles, accrued interest to the date of conversion is lost once the bonds are converted. Furthermore, on some convertibles, the dividend on the underlying shares for the same period may also be foregone. This can prove expensive, particularly if conversion is forced as a result of the issuer announcing early redemption (call).

None of these events affects a stock or bond portfolio. As a result, a convertible portfolio needs to be more actively managed.

The greater complexity of convertibles

Finally, convertibles are complex securities which require much time and effort to understand and appreciate fully, more so than their stock or bond counterparts. Some investors can be deterred by this; for those who do make the effort, however, the results are usually worthwhile.

Chapter 9

Summary and conclusions

Convertibles can make sense for all kinds of investors. They combine the best attributes of bonds and stocks, offering the long-term price appreciation of stocks with the income and capital preservation features of bonds. Provided the pitfalls and drawbacks have been properly evaluated, investors in stocks can benefit from adding convertibles, because in most markets most convertibles offer higher returns on a risk adjusted basis. Although in absolute terms the convertible's expected return is lower, once its lower risk is taken into account, its performance is superior. Equally, investors in bonds can benefit from owning convertibles in rising stock markets. The major pitfalls to convertible investing which can eliminate these attractions include a significant rise in long term interest rates, an unforeseen takeover bid and a decline in secondary market liquidity.

Part IV

Convertible valuation

Chapter 10

Convertible valuation

The purpose of this chapter is to provide both investors and issuers alike with an understanding of how convertibles are valued and how they behave in response to changes in share prices and interest rates. Investors will find this chapter helpful in assessing whether the market price of a convertible is cheap or expensive relative to its theoretical value. Issuers will find it helpful in understanding how new convertible issues are priced. The chapter outlines several techniques for calculating the theoretical value of a convertible, including concepts such as breakeven and discounted income advantage. Because most investors and nearly all issuers do not have access to computer based valuation models, all the valuation techniques used in this chapter are kept as simple as possible and can be implemented using a hand-held financial calculator.

The basic building blocks of convertible value

Financial theory suggests that the market price of any security which appeals to several different classes of investor should be the value ascribed to it by the class of investor that is prepared to pay the most for it. For convertibles, there are at least two classes of investor who are potential purchasers: investors in stocks, and investors in bonds. Determining which of these should be prepared to pay the most is the key to determining the convertible's theoretical value.

For stock investors, a convertible is worth at least its parity value (value if converted) since a convertible can always be converted into its underlying stock. The convertible should actually be worth more than this, since it also offers the additional benefits of a higher coupon than the yield on the stock, and the possibility of repayment of principal at final maturity. As a consequence, stock investors should be prepared to pay a premium over the convertible's parity value, where the premium represents the value to them of the extra income and redemption feature. Similarly, for bond investors, convertibles offer all the benefits of owning bonds in the company: they pay a regular coupon and guarantee redemption of principal at final maturity. In addition they also offer the benefit of the conversion option. As a consequence, bond investors should also be prepared to pay a premium over the convertible's intrinsic bond value.

Putting these two together, it is possible to say that a convertible's market value should be the higher of its value to stock investors or its value to bond investors. It may be even higher than this if convertible investors find it particularly attractive; however, its value to stock and bond investors establishes a floor below which, in theory, it should not fall. This can be expressed mathematically as follows:

$$\begin{aligned} \text{Theoretical value} &= \text{Higher of value to stock investors or bond investors.} \\ TV &= \text{Max } \{TV_s, TV_b\} \\ &= \text{Max } \{PV + P_s, BV + P_b\} \end{aligned}$$

Where

TV	=	Theoretical value of convertible.
TV_s	=	Theoretical value to stock investors.
TV_b	=	Theoretical value to bond investors.
PV	=	Parity value of convertible.
P_s	=	Premium over parity value payable by stock investors.
BV	=	Bond value of convertible.
P_b	=	Premium over bond value payable by bond investors.

Of course, in practice, convertibles do not always trade at theoretical value. Market imbalances often produce situations where a convertible is cheap or expensive relative to its fundamentals, i.e. situations where its theoretical value is above or below its market value. By comparing the convertible's market value with its theoretical value, the discerning investor can determine whether it is cheap or expensive.

Example

Throughout this chapter, the following example will be used. ABC Company has outstanding a fifteen year 7% conventional convertible with stated conversion price of $60. The convertible trades at 98% of par. ABC's shares trade at $50 and yield 4%. ABC's long-term (fifteen year) bonds yield 10½%. Is ABC's convertible cheap or expensive?

Much of the rest of this chapter focuses firstly on calculating the convertible's value to stock investors and secondly, on calculating its value to bond investors. The methods described are not as accurate as the best computer-based valuation models, but they have the advantage of being relatively simple to use and sufficiently near the mark that the user can derive a good sense of what the convertible is fundamentally worth.

Theoretical value to stock investors – TV_s

For stock investors, a convertible is worth its parity value plus a premium representing the value of the extra income and redemption feature offered in the period before conversion. Mathematically this is expressed as follows:

$TV_s = PV + P_s$

Calculating a convertible's parity value (PV) is relatively straightforward. It is the product of the convertible's conversion ratio and the current market price of the stock.

Parity value = Conversion ratio x share price

Example

For ABC's convertible:

Conversion ratio	=	$\dfrac{\text{Par value of bond}}{\text{Initial (stated) conversion price}}$
	=	$\dfrac{\$1{,}000}{\$60}$
	=	16.667 shares per $1,000 bond
Parity value	=	Conversion ratio × current share price
PV	=	16.667 × $50
	=	$833.33 per $1,000 bond
	=	83.3% of par

ABC's convertible has a parity value of 83%.

Calculating the convertible's premium (P_s) is harder. There are at least three methods which most market participants use: simple breakeven, adjusted breakeven and discounted income advantage. All three methods ignore the downside protection value of the convertible (i.e. its redemption feature), focusing exclusively on its income advantage. In this respect they are conservative, and the convertible is worth more than they suggest. Simple breakeven is the easiest method to use but is the most inaccurate. Adjusted breakeven is a little more complex, but slightly more accurate. Discounted income advantage is the most complex, but is the most accurate.

Simple breakeven

A convertible's breakeven is the number of years it takes for the stock investor buying the convertible instead of the stock to recoup the extra cost of the convertible (i.e. the premium) from the extra income (i.e. the difference between the coupon on the convertible and the dividend yield on the stock). Buying the convertible instead of the stock costs the stock investor a premium: in return for this, the stock investor earns extra income because the convertible's coupon exceeds the dividend yield on the stock. Breakeven measures the number of years it takes before the extra income from the convertible offsets the extra cost. As a result, breakeven is sometimes called payback. From the stock investor's perspective, the shorter the breakeven, the better. As a rule of thumb, most market participants expect a breakeven of no more than three years, except for very attractive convertibles (e.g. those issued by high quality blue-chip companies), where up to five years might be acceptable. Simple breakeven is the convertible's breakeven assuming that the income advantage of the convertible is merely the percentage difference between the convertible's coupon and the dividend yield on the stock:

$$\text{Simple breakeven} = \frac{\text{Premium required to purchase convertible}}{\text{Coupon} - \text{yield}}$$

$$= \frac{\text{Market price} - \text{parity value}}{\text{Coupon} - \text{yield}}$$

Example

For ABC's convertible:

Market price	=	98%
Parity value	=	83.3%
Coupon	=	7%
Yield	=	4%

Simple breakeven = $\dfrac{98\% - 83.3\%}{7\% - 4\%}$

= 4.9 years

When valuing convertibles, the breakeven formula can be reversed so that breakeven is used to determine the premium value of the convertible:

Premium = Breakeven × income advantage

P_s = Simple breakeven × (coupon − yield)

Example

For ABC's convertible:

P_s = Breakeven × (7% − 4%)
= 9% (three year breakeven)
to 15% (five year breakeven)

Using simple breakeven, ABC's convertible has a premium value to stock investors ranging from 9% to 15%, depending on whether stock investors are prepared to pay a three or five year simple breakeven. As a consequence, it has an overall value ranging from 92% to 98%, calculated as follows:

Theoretical value of convertible to stock investors
TV_s = Parity value + premium
= $PV + P_s$
= 83.3% + 9 to 15%
= 92% (three year breakeven)
98% (five year breakeven)

On the basis of this calculation, ABC's convertible has a market price at the top end of its theoretical value to stock investors.

Adjusted breakeven

Discerning investors will realise that the simple breakeven calculation outlined above is somewhat crude. In particular, it fails to recognise that the true income advantage from the convertible is not the percentage difference between the convertible's coupon and the stock's yield; rather it is the cash flow difference on a dollar for dollar basis taking into account the different market values in the convertible and the stock. When calculated on a dollar for dollar basis, the true income advantage of the convertible is as follows:

True income advantage = (Market price of convertible × coupon) − (market value of underlying shares × yield)
= (Market price of convertible × coupon) − (parity value of convertible × yield)

Example

For ABC's convertible:
Market price = 98%
Coupon = 7%
Parity value = 83.3%
Yield = 4%

True income advantage = (98% × 7%) − (83.3% × 4%)

True income advantage = 3.5%

Adjusted breakeven is simple breakeven adjusted for the true income advantage of the convertible as follows:

$$\text{Adjusted breakeven} = \frac{\text{Premium required to purchase convertible}}{\text{True income advantage}}$$

Example

For ABC's convertible:

$$\text{Adjusted breakeven} = \frac{98\% - 83.3\%}{3.5\%}$$

= 4.2 years

The adjusted breakeven of 4.2 years compares with a simple breakeven of 4.9 years for the same convertible. Since it is more accurate, adjusted breakeven is closer to the mark.

Reversing the formula, the convertible's premium value to stock investors can be calculated as follows:

Premium	=	Adjusted breakeven × true income advantage
P_s	=	Adjusted breakeven × (MV × C − PV × D)

Where

MV	=	Market value of convertible (% of par)
C	=	Coupon on convertible (%)
PV	=	Parity value (% of par)
D	=	Dividend yield on stock (%)

Example

For ABC's convertible:

MV	=	98%
C	=	7%
PV	=	83.3%
D	=	4%

So:

P_s	=	Adjusted breakeven × (MV × C − PV × D)
	=	Adjusted breakeven × 3.5%
	=	10.5% (three year breakeven)
	to	17.5% (five year breakeven)

Using adjusted breakeven, and adding the premium to the convertible's parity value, ABC's convertible has a theoretical value to stock investors ranging from 94% (three year breakeven) to 101% (five year breakeven). On the basis of its market price of 98%, it appears fairly valued.

Discounted income advantage

In the same way that adjusted breakeven compensated for shortcomings in the simple breakeven calculation at the cost of an increase in complexity, so the discounted income advantage calculation compensates for shortcomings in the adjusted breakeven calculation at the cost of even greater complexity.

There are two drawbacks with the simple and adjusted breakeven models: the convertible yield advantage is assumed to be constant throughout the breakeven period, and no account is taken of the time value of money. Of course, in reality, neither assumption is correct: while the income from owning the convertible remains fixed, that from owning the underlying shares will change in line with changes in the company's dividends, and in all probability will increase as the dividends grow. In addition, the premium required to own the convertible is paid up-front while the income advantage is recouped later. If account were taken of the time value of money, the income advantage of the convertible would be reduced on a present value basis.

The discounted income advantage calculation reflects both changing dividends and the time value of money, as follows. First, it projects future dividend income from owning the shares under different assumed dividend growth rates. Second, it calculates the yield advantage of the convertible in each year of the projection under each dividend growth scenario. Third, it terminates the projection at the point where the income advantage from the convertible turns negative, i.e. when dividends have grown to the point where the income from the shares exceeds the coupon on the bond. (At this point, stock investors are assumed to convert the convertible into its underlying shares to take advantage of the extra yield.) Finally it discounts to present value the convertible's yield advantage up to the crossover point. The convertible's premium value to stock investors is then determined to be this present value number.

Example

For ABC's convertible:
Parity value = 83.3%
= $833.33 per $1,000 bond
Dividend on underlying
shares in year one = 4% of parity value
= 4% of $833.33
= $33.33 per $1,000 bond
Coupon on convertible = 7%
= $70 per $1,000 bond

Assuming dividends grow at a 10% or 15% annual rate, the income advantage cash flows would be as follows:

CONVERTIBLE VALUATION

| | 10% dividend growth ||| 15% dividend growth |||
Year	Coupon on convertible	Dividend on shares	Income advantage	Coupon on convertible	Dividend on shares	Income advantage
1	$70	$33.33	$36.67	$70	$33.33	$36.67
2	$70	$36.67	$33.33	$70	$38.33	$31.67
3	$70	$40.33	$29.67	$70	$44.08	$25.92
4	$70	$44.37	$25.63	$70	$50.70	$19.30
5	$70	$48.80	$21.20	$70	$58.30	$11.70
6	$70	$53.68	$16.32	$70	$67.05	$2.95
7	$70	$59.05	$10.95	$70	$77.10	—
8	$70	$64.96	$5.04	$70	$88.67	—
9	$70	$71.45	—	$70	$101.97	—
	Net present value at 10%		$131.02 = 13.1% of par	Net present value at 10%		$101.10 = 10.1% of par

If ABC's dividends grow at a 10 to 15% annual rate, this calculation suggests that the premium value to stock investors of ABC's convertible is between 10.1% and 13.1% of par. Given a parity value of 83.3%, this implies that ABC's convertible would be worth between 93% and 96% to stock investors.

Summary: theoretical value to stock investors – TV_S

A convertible's theoretical value to stock investors is the sum of its parity value plus a premium representing the value of the convertible's extra income and downside protection. Most calculations of premium are conservative: they ignore the value of the downside protection and focus exclusively on the convertible's income advantage instead. There are three commonly used methods to calculate income advantage: in increasing order of complexity, they are simple breakeven, adjusted breakeven, and discounted income advantage.

Mathematically, the convertible's theoretical value can be expressed as follows:

Theoretical value to stock investors = Parity value + Premium
TV_S = $PV + P_S$

Where

Parity value (PV) = Conversion ratio × share price
Premium (P_S) =
(1) Simple breakeven × (coupon − yield); or
(2) Adjusted breakeven × true income advantage; or
(3) Net present value of income advantage.

Example

For ABC's convertible:

$PV + P_S$	=	92% to 98% (simple breakeven)
	or	94% to 101% (adjusted breakeven)
	or	93% to 96% (discounted income advantage)
Average value	=	Approximately 96%

All these calculations suggest that at 98%, ABC's convertible trades above the average of its value to stock investors. Part or all this is likely to be attributable to the value of the downside protection, which all three calculations ignore.

Theoretical value to bond investors - TV_b

For bond investors, a convertible must be worth at least its value as a straight bond, i.e. its value as a bond without the conversion option, plus the value of the conversion option. Mathematically, this is expressed as follows:

$$TV_b = BV + P_b$$

Where

BV = Value of convertible as a straight bond
P_b = Value of conversion option

Calculating the convertible's bond value (BV) is relatively straightforward. It is the discounted present value of the convertible's coupons and principal at a discount rate equal to the yield on straight bonds of a similar maturity and credit risk.

Example

For ABC's convertible:
Appropriate discount rate = 10½%

Year	Cash flow per $1,000 bond
1	$70
2	$70
3	$70
4	$70
5	$70
6	$70
7	$70
8	$70
9	$70
10	$70
11	$70

CONVERTIBLE VALUATION

12	$70
13	$70
14	$70
15	$1,070

Net present value at 10½% = $741.22
= 74.1% of par

ABC's convertible has a bond value of 74.1%

Calculating the premium (P_b) is more complex. One method sometimes used is to consider the convertible as a package of a straight bond with an equity warrant, where the equity warrant can be exercised only by tendering the bond. The straight bond has a value equivalent to the convertible's bond value. The equity warrant has a value equivalent to the premium which bond investors should pay for the convertible's conversion option. For a convertible considered in this fashion, determining the value of the equity warrant is the key to determining the value of the premium. Different markets have different techniques for valuing equity warrants. The world's largest bond with equity warrant market, the Euromarket, assesses the value of an equity warrant by reference to its overall premium and gearing, which are defined as follows:

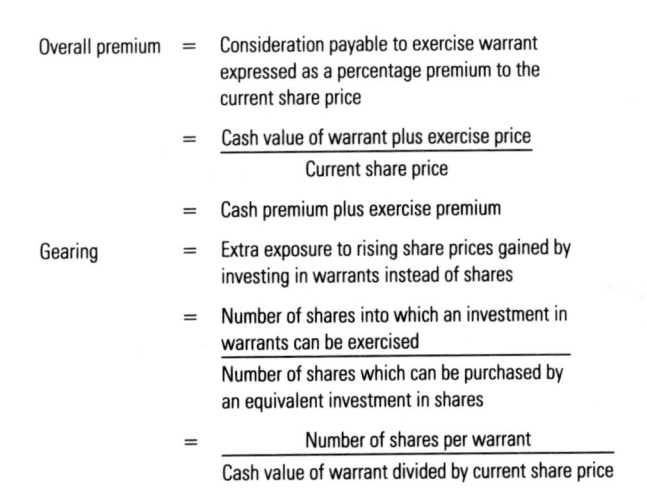

Overall premium = Consideration payable to exercise warrant expressed as a percentage premium to the current share price

= $\dfrac{\text{Cash value of warrant plus exercise price}}{\text{Current share price}}$

= Cash premium plus exercise premium

Gearing = Extra exposure to rising share prices gained by investing in warrants instead of shares

= $\dfrac{\text{Number of shares into which an investment in warrants can be exercised}}{\text{Number of shares which can be purchased by an equivalent investment in shares}}$

= $\dfrac{\text{Number of shares per warrant}}{\text{Cash value of warrant divided by current share price}}$

The most attractive warrants, i.e. warrants for which Euromarket investors will pay the highest cash premium over their intrinsic value, are those which have a combination of low overall premium and high gearing. Low overall premium is attractive because the cost of buying shares through exercise of the warrants is low relative to the cost of buying shares directly. High gearing is attractive because the profit potential from owning the warrant is highest. Gearing is a measure of exposure to changing stock prices: for every dollar change in share prices, the intrinsic value of an equivalent investment in warrants will change by the same amount multiplied by the gearing factor. For bullish investors, the higher the gearing, the greater the profit potential from the warrant relative to the stock, and the more attractive the warrant.

In practice, the most attractive warrants, i.e. those with the best combination of low overall premium and high gearing, tend to be warrants which are either at the money or slightly in the money. Warrants which are far out of the money have a high overall premium and are unattractive. Warrants which are deep in the money have a low gearing (because the cost of the warrant has to include the warrant's intrinsic value and is therefore high relative to the shares) and are equally unattractive. As a result, Euromarket investors typically pay the highest cash premium over intrinsic value for warrants which are at the money or up to 10% in the money; in this range, the premium which investors pay over the warrant's intrinsic value can be as much as 20–25% of the underlying share price. Warrants which are further out of or in the money than this are worth less, i.e. investors pay a lower cash premium over intrinsic value. This can be summarised as follows:

Euromarket Warrant Valuation Table

Warrant exercise premium[1]	In or out of the money	Approximate market price of warrant[1]
20% and over	Out	1 to 5%
10%	Out	10%
Zero	—	20%
−10%	In	20% plus intrinsic value
−20%	In	10% plus intrinsic value
−30% and under	In	1 to 5% plus intrinsic value

Note: [1]Expressed as a percentage of its underlying share price.

The Euromarket warrant valuation table can be used to calculate the bond premium (B_p) in a convertible, as follows. Treating the convertible as a package of a bond with an equity warrant, the equivalent of the exercise price of the warrant is the bond value of the convertible. This is because the warrant can be exercised only by tendering the bond, and the value of the consideration payable on exercise of the warrant is the market value of the bond. The market value of the bond is, of course, the convertible's bond value. Correspondingly, the equivalent of the current share price of the warrant is the convertible's parity value, because the convertible's parity value measures the market value of the consideration received on exercise of the warrant, i.e. the equivalent of the current share price. Finally, the equivalent of the cash value of the warrant is the convertible's bond premium (B_p) Mathematically, this can be expressed as follows:

Exercise price	=	Bond value
	=	BV
Exercise premium	=	Bond value of convertible expressed as a percentage premium to its parity value.
	=	BV–PV
		PV
Intrinsic value	=	Equivalent of current share price minus warrant exercise price, when share price exceeds exercise price.
	=	Parity value of convertible minus bond value.
	=	PV–BV

The Euromarket warrant valuation table can then be re-expressed for convertibles as follows:

Premium Value of Convertible to Bond Investors

Convertible exercise premium	Approximate bond premium
BV–PV	
PV	B_p
20% and over	1 to 5% of PV
10%	10% of PV
Zero	20% of PV
–10%	20% of PV plus PV–BV
–20%	10% of PV plus PV–BV
–30% and under	1 to 5% of PV plus PV–BV

Example

For ABC's convertible:

BV	=	74.1%
PV	=	83.3%
Exercise price	=	BV
	=	74.1%

Exercise premium $= \dfrac{BV-PV}{PV}$

$= \dfrac{74.1\% - 83.3\%}{83.3\%}$

$= -11.1\%$

ABC's convertible is 11.1% in the money. As a consequence, using the warrant valuation table above, the warrant must be worth approximately 20% of the convertible's parity value plus its intrinsic value, as follows:

B_p = 20% of parity value plus intrinsic value

= 20% of PV plus PV−BV

= (20% × 83.3%) + (83.3%−74.1%)

= 25.9%

Consequently, to a bond investor, ABC's convertible is worth 100%, calculated as follows:

Value to bond investor = $BV + B_p$

= 74.1% + 25.9%

= 100.0%

When compared with its market value of 98%, ABC's convertible looks relatively inexpensive for a bond investor.

Putting the building blocks together

The convertible's theoretical value is the higher of its value to stock investors and its value to bond investors

TV = Max(TV_s, TV_b)
TV_s = $PV + P_s$
TV_b = $BV + P_b$

PV = Parity value.
P_s = Premium to stock investors calculated using simple breakeven, adjusted breakeven or discounted income advantage models.
BV = Bond value.
P_b = Premium to bond investors calculated by considering convertibles as a package of a bond with a warrant, and valuing warrant component in accordance with prevailing prices for equity warrants.

Example

For ABC's convertible:

Value to stock investors	=	96% (average valuation, conservatively ignoring benefit of downside protection)
Value to bond investors	=	100%
Theoretical market value	=	Higher of value to stock or bond investors
	=	100%
Actual market price	=	98%

ABC's convertible appears relatively inexpensive relative to its calculated theoretical value.

Changes in underlying share price

Using the methods outlined above, or any other valuation methods, it is possible to plot the theoretical value of a convertible against changes in its underlying share price. The results of such a plot are illustrated graphically in Exhibit 10.1. The convertible's price behaviour illustrates its principal investment attraction: the combination of long run upside potential through growth in the underlying share price, together with the income advantage and downside protection feature of bonds. Share price C is the share price which would typically prevail at the launch of a convertible offering. At this point the convertible is worth more than its parity or bond value, the premium being calculated in accordance with one of the valuation formulae. If all works well and the company's share price appreciates over time towards D, the convertible will also appreciate in value, although the premium over parity value will decline in line with the decline in value of the downside protection feature.

If, however, the stock market falls or the company does not produce good results, and the share price declines towards B, then the convertible's value will be held up by its bond value – the capital preservation feature. Again the premium over bond value will decline, reflecting the declining value of the conversion option. If the share price declines below B towards A, then this is probably because the company itself is in business or financial difficulty, in which case the value of the company's bonds, including the convertible, is also likely to decline.

Changes in interest rates

A similar graph illustrating the theoretical value of a convertible against changes in interest rates is illustrated in Exhibit 10.2. It

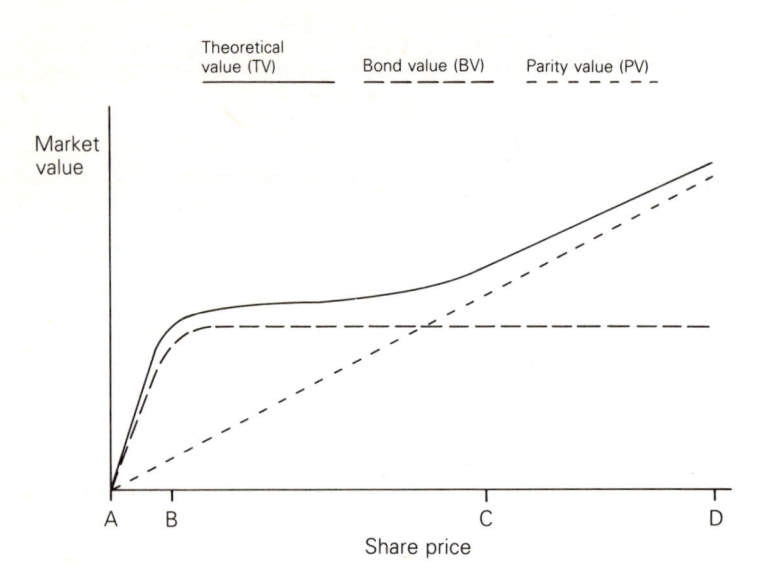

Exhibit 10.1 Market value analysis against share price

shows that the convertible again enjoys most of the upside potential of bonds in a falling interest rate environment, with a degree of protection against the downside of rising interest rates. Interest rates at point B are those typically prevailing at launch. Were interest rates to decline significantly towards point A, the convertible's value would rise in line with rises in the value of the company's bonds. Equally, a precipitous rise in interest rates towards point C produces a decline in the value of the convertible, although there is a floor on the downside represented by the convertible's parity value.

Pitfalls in convertible valuation

A convertible's value depends on a number of external factors. An unforeseen rise in interest rates, or an unexpected takeover bid, or a decline in secondary market liquidity can all lead to significant variations in the convertible's market value from its theoretical value. The effects of these are all illustrated in the third part of this book on investing in convertibles, but should be fully taken into account in assessing the convertible's value. Two other factors internal to the convertible are examined here.

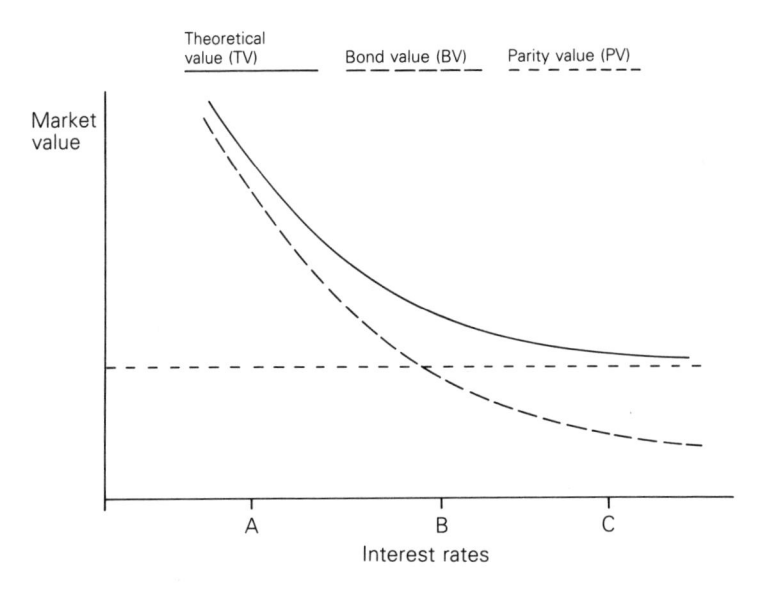

Exhibit 10.2 Market value analysis against interest rates

Call features

Before any attempt is made to value the convertible, it is essential to examine closely its call features. Most convertibles in the major convertible markets of the world are callable at the issuer's option, usually at any time after a non-call period of three to five years from launch. Some convertibles are callable even earlier, although there is usually a precondition with respect to a minimum level for the company's share price before the call can be operated. The purpose of such call flexibility is to allow the issuer to force investors to convert their holdings into equity by calling the bonds as soon as the convertible's parity value exceeds its redemption value.

As soon as a convertible becomes callable, and assuming that the convertible's parity value exceeds its bond value, its premium over parity value is likely to contract significantly because the convertible's breakeven will be limited to the time period between announcement of a call and the actual payment date — usually no more than thirty days. In addition the convertible's bond value is likely to be affected by call features; no matter what the level of interest rates, the bond value can never rise above the call price.

Put features

The inclusion of investor put features also significantly affects the convertible's value, although this time in favour of the investor. A put can significantly shorten the effective life of the convertible, with positive benefits for its bond value; this should be calculated assuming the put is exercised. On the other hand, careful consideration also needs to be given as to whether or not the put may be exercised when performing breakeven or income advantage calculations.

Conclusion

No method for predicting a convertible's value is perfect. Ultimately only market forces determine it. However, in the absence of computer models, the methods outlined in this chapter will help the discerning investor derive a good sense of what a convertible is fundamentally worth.

Part V

The principal markets

Chapter 11

❖

Overview of the Euromarket

The purpose of this chapter is to provide an overview of the Euromarket for both prospective issuers and investors. The chapter reviews recent trends in new issue activity in order to illustrate the types of issues undertaken, and describes the structure and terms of a typical Euroconvertible. It concludes with a section for investors on trading and settlement procedures.

Whether measured by new issue activity, or the depth and sophistication of the market, the Euromarket is one of the more important markets in the world. Outside Japan, it is one of the world's largest (see Exhibit 11.1). Ease of access and an increasingly sophisticated investor base attract issuers, while investors are drawn by the variety of issues on offer from a large number of different borrowers from different countries.

Types of issue

There are two principal types of Euroconvertible:

1. Conventional convertibles.
2. Convertibles with early redemption (put) options for the investor.

Exhibit 11.2 gives a breakdown of new issue activity in each type of security in 1988, and for comparison, new issue activity in the other type of hybrid equity security, bonds with equity warrants. The depth of the Euromarket can be seen from the total of new issue activity which in 1988 was the equivalent of approximately US$ 34 billion. Measured by this yardstick, the Euromarket is the largest hybrid equity market in the world outside Japan. Of

New issue volume in 1988

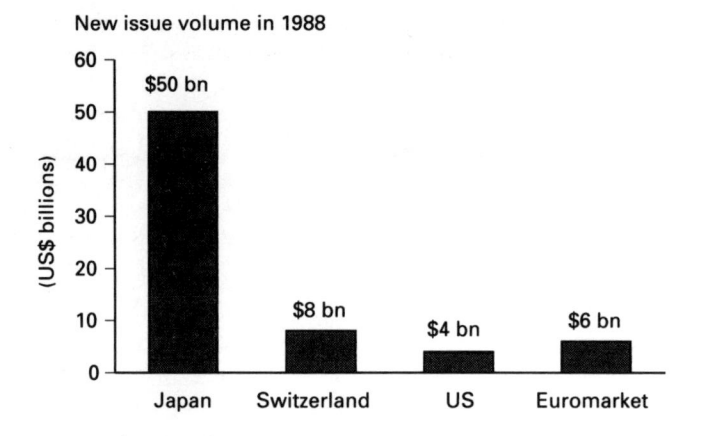

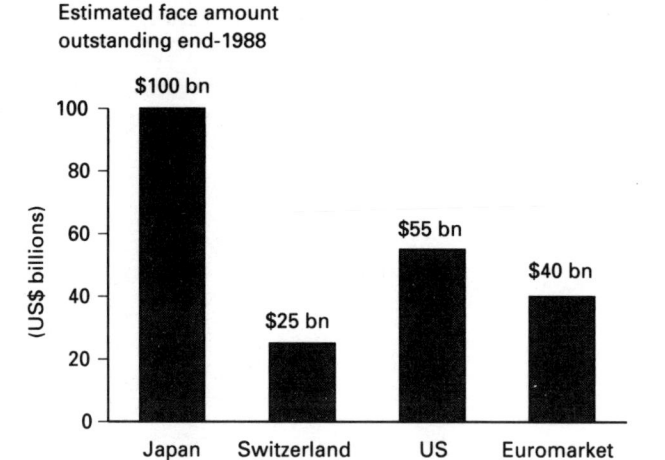

Japan	$50 bn
Switzerland	$8 bn
US	$4 bn
Euromarket	$6 bn

Estimated face amount outstanding end-1988

Japan	$100 bn
Switzerland	$25 bn
US	$55 bn
Euromarket	$40 bn

Exhibit 11.1 Comparison of the world's major convertible markets

significance, perhaps, is the fact that new issue activity is several orders of magnitude greater than that in the United States.

Approximately 83% of new issue volume ($28 billion) was in the form of bonds with equity warrants: of this, more than 95% ($27 billion) was from Japanese companies. By comparison convertible issuance by Japanese entities totalled less than $1 billion. The principal reason for the greater use of bonds with warrants by Japanese companies was the companies' wish to currency swap the interest and principal of the security, usually denominated in US dollars, back into yen, and thereby achieve extremely low cost fixed-rate yen financing. A yen denominated convertible would not have been as cheap, and a convertible in a currency other than yen cannot be swapped into yen without the borrower incurring considerable foreign exchange risk (because of the uncertainty over the conversion date of the convertible).

Approximately 8% of new issue volume ($3 billion) was in the form of puttable convertibles. With the exception of some Japanese convertible issues in the 1970s, put options in convertibles were rare until about 1984 or 1985. Always popular with investors, issuers had been reluctant to offer them unless there was a *quid pro quo*, usually in the form of a lower coupon. The creation of the rolling or flexible put in early 1988 (described in Part II), which significantly increases the probability that a puttable convertible will be converted, has made companies more willing to offer puts, with the result that there has been a significant increase in the use of this type of convertible in the last few years.

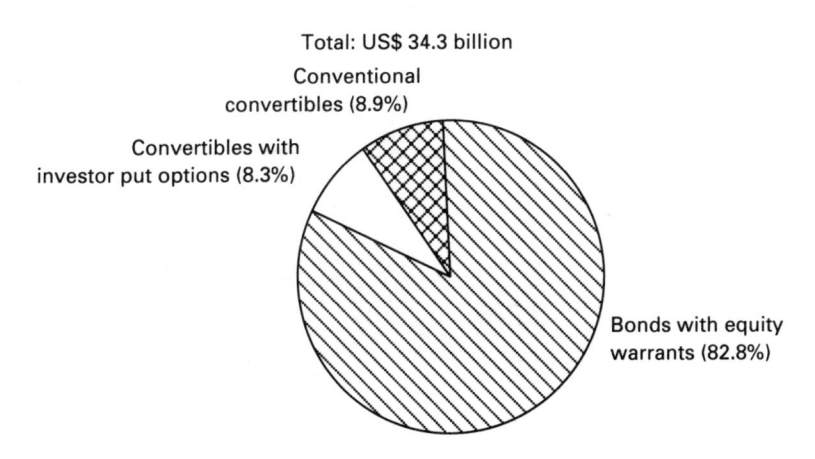

Exhibit 11.2 Hybrid securities issued in the Euromarket in 1988 (*Source*: Euromoney Bondware)

Growth of the Euroconvertible market

Exhibit 11.3 illustrates the growth in new issue activity over the last five years for convertibles only (i.e. excluding bonds with warrants), and for comparison, similar figures for the US domestic market. With new issue activity in convertibles alone matching that of the United States in the last few years, the graph again illustrates the depth of the Euromarket.

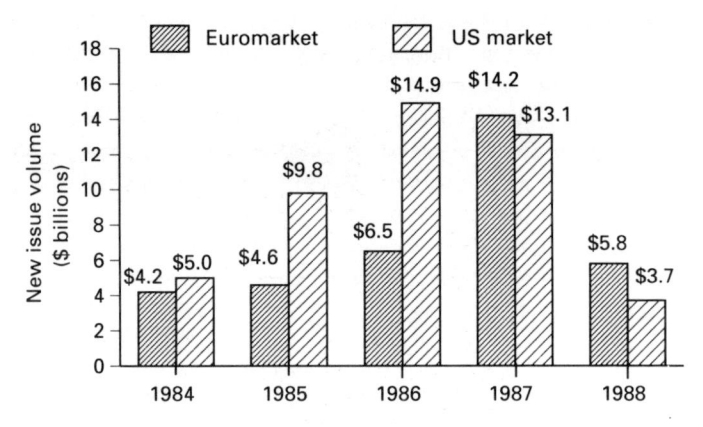

Exhibit 11.3 Growth of the convertible markets 1984–8 (*Source*: Euromoney Bondware)

New issue volume in both markets slumped dramatically after the stock market crash of October 1987. The decline was not due to lack of investor demand – far from it: most new issues in 1988 and 1989 were successfully distributed and more issues could have been launched, had companies been willing. Most companies, however, seemed to prefer to wait on the sidelines rather than sell potential equity at prices which in most cases were still well below levels prevailing just before the crash.

Nationality of issuers

Exhibit 11.4 provides a breakdown over the last three years of the different nationalities of companies which have issued in the Euromarket. No other market in the world offers such a variety of different borrowers from different countries.

Over the past few years, there has been a substantial decline in activity by the traditional users of the market: US and Japanese companies. US companies have fallen out of favour with investors over the last few years because of the substantial decline in the US dollar; despite the considerable appreciation in the US stock market, the gains in share prices have often been insufficient to offset the currency loss. Japanese issuers are now primarily banks; companies which used to issue convertibles have switched their issuing activity into bonds with equity warrants, where the associated currency swap into fixed-rate yen produces a cost of funds well below that achievable on a convertible.

1986
Total: US$ 6.5 bn

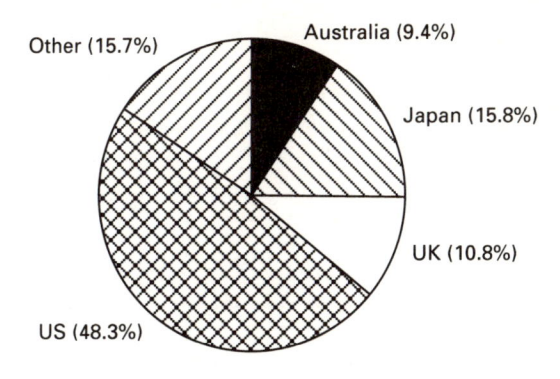

- Other (15.7%)
- Australia (9.4%)
- Japan (15.8%)
- UK (10.8%)
- US (48.3%)

1987
Total: US$ 14.2bn

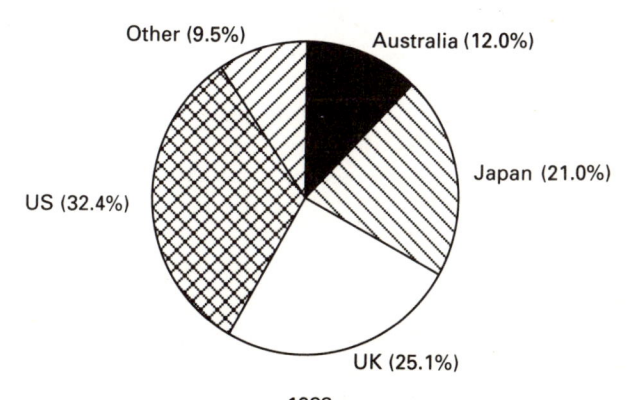

- Other (9.5%)
- Australia (12.0%)
- Japan (21.0%)
- UK (25.1%)
- US (32.4%)

1988
Total: US$ 5.8bn

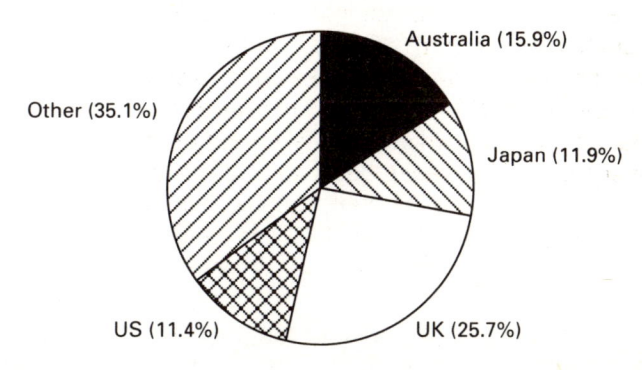

- Other (35.1%)
- Australia (15.9%)
- Japan (11.9%)
- UK (25.7%)
- US (11.4%)

Exhibit 11.4 Euromarket new issue volume analysed by nationality 1986–8 (*Source*: Euromoney Bondware)

Correspondingly, there has been an increase in the use of the market by non-traditional issuers, particularly UK and Australian companies, and more recently continental European companies. In 1988, for example, there were issues from companies in Sweden, France, Switzerland, Holland, Spain, Portugal and Italy. These have all proved popular with investors, primarily because of the strength of the underlying stock markets. The trend towards non-traditional issuers looks set to continue as investors seek to diversify and reduce risk, and issuers seek new sources of capital.

Date	Issuer	Amount
Mar. 1984	Texaco	$1,000m
Apr. 1984	Texaco	$ 500m
Jan. 1986	W.R. Grace	$ 250m
Feb. 1986	IBM (convertible into Intel)	$ 300m
May 1986	Eastman Kodak	$ 300m
Jun. 1986	Viacom	$ 225m
Sep. 1986	Rorer	$ 250m
Sep. 1986	Chubb	$ 200m
Mar. 1987	CBS	$ 400m
May 1987	American Brands	$ 400m
Aug. 1987	MCA	$ 300m
Aug. 1987	International Paper	$ 200m
Aug. 1987	Texas Instruments	$ 300m
Aug. 1988	American Brands	$ 200m
Sep. 1989	MCA	$ 200m

Exhibit 11.5 Selected US issuers of Euroconvertibles

Date	Issuer	Amount
Feb. 1987	Asda–MFI	£110m
Feb. 1987	Redland	£120m
Mar. 1987	Tesco	£115m
Apr. 1987	Consolidated Gold Fields	£110m
Jul. 1987	Hillsdown Holdings	£150m
Aug. 1987	Grand Metropolitan	£100m
Sep. 1987	Next	£100m
Mar. 1988	United Biscuits	£110m
Apr. 1988	Slough Estates	£150m
Jun. 1988	Saatchi & Saatchi	£176m
Jan. 1989	Thorn EMI	£103m
Mar. 1989	J. Sainsbury	£150m
May 1989	Ladbroke	£150m
Jun. 1989	United Newspapers (convertible into Reuters)	£105m
Jul. 1989	Land Securities	£175m

Exhibit 11.6 Selected UK issuers of Euroconvertibles

Exhibits 11.5 to 11.9 give examples of recent Euroconvertibles issued by US, UK, European, Japanese and Australasian companies. Of particular significance, perhaps, is the increasing presence of companies which are not well known household names (see Exhibit 11.10). It used to be the case that Euromarket investors would buy only the securities of companies they knew, with the result that potential issuers were restricted to only the largest and best known of US and Japanese names. Today, however, the investor base has become increasingly institutional: the proverbial Belgian dentist, the mainstay of the Eurobond market in the 1960s and 1970s, now accounts for a more modest contribution to overall investment activity. Private banks, money

Date	Issuer	Country	Amount	US$ equivalent
Jan. 1987	Bank Julius Baer	Switzerland	DM 150m	$ 82m
May 1987	L.M. Ericsson	Sweden	$60m	$ 60m
Apr. 1988	Inspectorate	Switzerland	£69m	$131m
May 1988	Center Parcs	Netherlands	£60m	$113m
Jun. 1988	Lafarge Coppee	France	FF 1,520m	$262m
Jun. 1988	Torras Hostench	Spain	£100m	$182m
Jun. 1988	Cie. Generale d'Electricite	France	ECU 250m	$284m
Jun. 1988	CIR	Italy	Lit 125bn	$ 93m
Jul. 1988	Telefonica	Spain	$200m	$200m
Jul. 1988	Michelin	France	FF 1,500m	$243m
Jul. 1988	Espirito Santo	Portugal	$100m	$100m
Dec. 1988	Svenska Cellulosa	Sweden	ECU 101m	$120m
Jun. 1989	Arbed	Luxembourg	ECU 65m	$ 69m
Jul. 1989	Merloni	Italy	Lit 100bn	$ 72m

Exhibit 11.7 Selected continental European issuers of Euroconvertibles

Date	Issuer	Amount
Apr. 1986	Sumitomo Trust	$150m
Feb. 1987	Omron Tateisi	$150m
Jul. 1987	Long-Term Credit Bank	$200m
Jul. 1987	Mitsubishi Bank	$300m
Sep. 1987	Sanwa Bank	$300m
Oct. 1987	Fuji Bank	$200m
Feb. 1988	Mitsui Bank	$200m
Jan. 1989	Sumitomo Bank	$300m and DM300m
Apr. 1989	Mitsubishi Bank	$300m and DM500m
May 1989	Dai-Ichi Kangyo Bank	$300m and DM200m
Oct. 1989	Mitsubishi Trust	DM300m

Exhibit 11.8 Selected Japanese issuers of Euroconvertibles

Date	Issuer	Amount	US$ equivalent
Jan. 1987	Elders	$75m, £85m, DM150m and Hfl100m	$338m
Mar. 1987	Bell Group	A$175m	$120m
May 1987	Bell Resources	$200m	$200m
May 1987	Mount Isa Mines	$125m and A$125m	$214m
Jun. 1987	Goodman Fielder	£85m	$138m
Jun. 1987	Bond Corp	£80m and $200m	$330m
Jul. 1987	Coles Myer	A$125m	$ 90m
Feb. 1988	News Corp (exchangeable into Pearson)	$150m	$150m
Mar. 1988	Bond Corp (exchangeable into Allied Lyons)	£125m	$221m
May 1988	Pioneer Concrete	A$175m	$138m
Jun. 1988	Bond Corp (exchangeable into Allied Lyons)	£104m	$193m
Jun. 1988	TNT	A$175m	$143m
Oct. 1988	Fletcher Challenge	$75m	$ 75m
Feb. 1989	News Corp (exchangeable into Pearson)	£150m, DM175m and Hfl100m	$400m

Exhibit 11.9 Selected Australasian issuers of Euroconvertibles

Date	Issuer	Nationality	Amount	US$ equivalent
Jan. 1988	Wilson Sporting Goods	US	$ 10m	$ 10m
Apr. 1988	Comcast	US	$100m	$100m
Apr. 1988	Cellular Communications	US	$ 50m	$ 50m
Jun. 1988	Meggitt Holdings	UK	£ 17m	$ 30m
Jul. 1988	Vishay Intertechnology	US	$ 50m	$ 50m
Jul. 1988	Thermo Instruments	US	$ 30m	$ 30m
Sep. 1988	Saehan Media	South Korea	$ 30m	$ 30m
Nov. 1988	Health Images	US	$ 15m	$ 15m
Dec. 1988	Dawson International	UK	£ 30m	$ 56m
Jan. 1989	Albert Fisher	UK	£ 37m	$ 65m

Exhibit 11.10 Selected 'Emerging Growth' issuers of Euroconvertibles

management firms, mutual funds, pension funds and life insurance companies are now the predominant investors. With the growth of institutionalisation has come sophistication, and growing ability on the part of the investor base to recognise and understand good investment opportunities. This has opened the market to companies which may previously have been unknown to Euromarket investors, but which nevertheless offer attractive investment opportunities.

Currency of issue

The Euromarket is unique among convertible markets because currency, or more precisely the expected future performance of the currency on the foreign exchange markets, plays a key part in investors' decisions as to what to purchase. By and large, only convertibles denominated in currencies that investors perceive to be strong will be invested in: weak currencies stand the chance of being rejected, notwithstanding the strength of the underlying stock market. This is illustrated in Exhibit 11.11, which provides a breakdown of new issue volume by currency in the past few years. The effects of the weakness of the US dollar over this period are shown clearly: from being historically the most important currency of issue and investment, with more than 86% of 1986's new issue volume denominated in US dollars, the currency has declined in importance to the point where in 1988 it ranked second to sterling. The growth in the use of sterling reflects the same phenomenon, but with exactly the opposite effects. Investors were willing to purchase more sterling denominated securities during this period because the currency was perceived to be strong.

Future issuing and investment activity will again depend on which currencies are strong, with one exception: the US dollar. No matter how weak, it is likely that the US dollar will never decline to insignificance while it remains the major reserve currency in the world. No matter what their country of origin, most Euromarket investors will always have a proportion of their assets denominated in dollars.

Typical convertible issue

Average size

The Euromarket is capable of accommodating some very large (up to $1 billion) convertible issues, as well as some very small ones ($10 million or less), as Exhibits 11.12 and 11.13 illustrate. On average, however, the size of a typical issue has been around $100 million (see Exhibit 11.14). Exhibit 11.14 also illustrates that the average size has been increasing in the last few years. This reflects both the increasing ability of the market to accommodate large issues and also investor preference for larger, more liquid, transactions.

THE PRINCIPAL MARKETS

1986
Total: US$ 6.5 billion

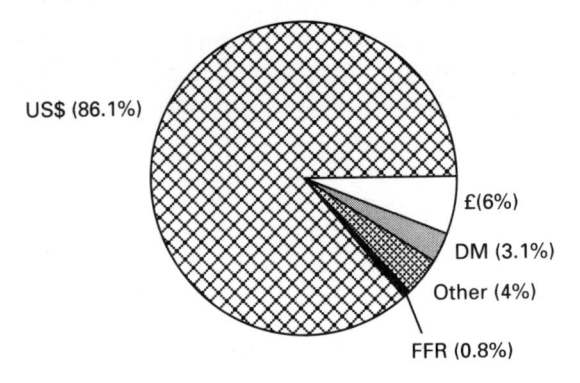

- US$ (86.1%)
- £ (6%)
- DM (3.1%)
- Other (4%)
- FFR (0.8%)

1987
Total: US$ 14.2 billion

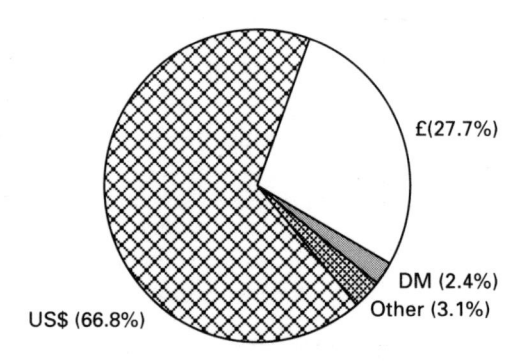

- US$ (66.8%)
- £ (27.7%)
- DM (2.4%)
- Other (3.1%)

1988
Total: US$ 5.8 billion

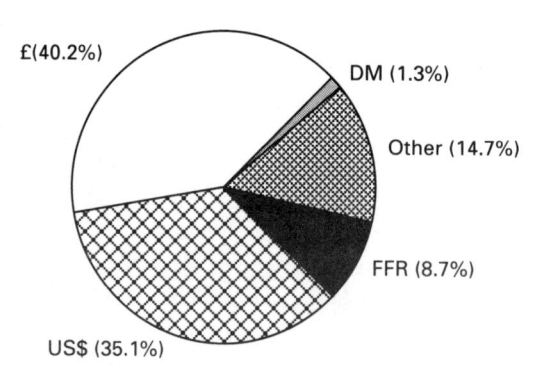

- £ (40.2%)
- DM (1.3%)
- Other (14.7%)
- FFR (8.7%)
- US$ (35.1%)

Exhibit 11.11 Euromarket new issue volume analysed by currency (*Source*: Euromoney Bondware)

Date	Issuer	Country	Amount
Mar. 1984	Texaco	US	$1,000m
May 1989	Dai-Ichi Kangyo Bank	Japan	$ 977m*
Jan. 1989	Sumitomo Bank	Japan	$ 935m*
Apr. 1989	Mitsubishi Bank	Japan	$ 566m*
Sep. 1985	Rockefeller Center Properties	US	$ 550m*
Apr. 1984	Texaco	US	$ 500m
Oct. 1986	Elders	Australia	$ 453m*
Feb. 1989	Bank of Tokyo	Japan	$ 420m*
Jan. 1987	Elders	Australia	$ 423m*
Oct. 1986	Bell Resources	Australia	$ 410m*

Note: *Multi-tranche issues

Exhibit 11.12 The largest Euroconvertible issues

Date	Issuer	Country	Amount
Aug. 1985	Pegasus Gold	Canada	$ 6.6 million
Aug. 1982	Tokyu Corporation	Japan	$ 8.5 million
Jan. 1988	Wilson Sporting Goods	US	$10 million
Apr. 1981	Hexcel	US	$10 million
Sep. 1980	Huffy	US	$10 million
Mar. 1985	Choguku Marine Paints	Japan	$10 million
Feb. 1982	Trans-Western Exploration	US	$10 million
Jun. 1982	SCI Systems	US	$12 million
Jul. 1981	Texas General Resources	US	$12 million
Jul. 1983	Ferrofluid Capital	US	$12.5 million
Apr. 1982	Asics Corp	Japan	$12.5 million
Jan. 1981	Anacomp	US	$12.5 million

Exhibit 11.13 The smallest Euroconvertible issues

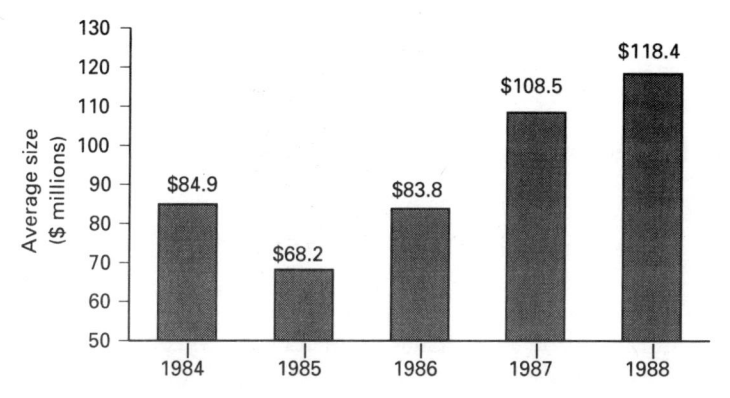

Average size ($ millions):
- 1984: $84.9
- 1985: $68.2
- 1986: $83.8
- 1987: $108.5
- 1988: $118.4

Exhibit 11.14 Average size of new issues in the Euromarket 1984–8 (*Source*: Euromoney Bondware)

One feature that is not illustrated in Exhibit 11.14 is the trade off, for prospective issuers, of size against cost. At the bottom end of the spectrum, the smallest issues suffer from being illiquid, or difficult to trade, so that investors require more generous terms from the issuer to compensate. At the other end of the spectrum, the largest issues are difficult to place unless the terms are sufficiently generous to increase overall demand. As a result, the finest terms are commanded by issues with a size somewhere in the middle. This is typically acknowledged to be somewhere between $100 million and $250 million.

Maturity

Most Euroconvertible issues have a final maturity of fifteen years, as Exhibit 11.15 illustrates, although there are a considerable number of ten year transactions. Investor put options on some Euroconvertible issues may serve to shorten the effective maturity to as little as the first put date, generally five years.

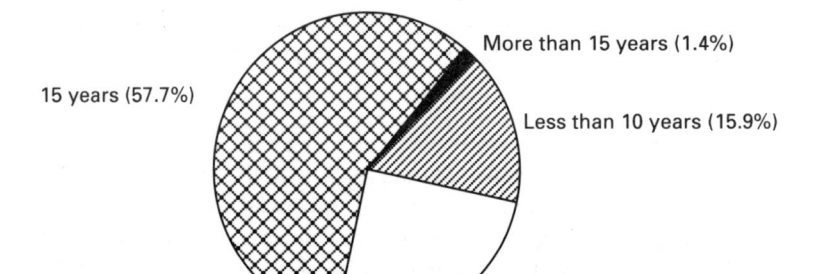

Total: US$ 5.8 billion

15 years (57.7%)
More than 15 years (1.4%)
Less than 10 years (15.9%)
10 years (24.9%)

Exhibit 11.15 Euromarket maturity profile of new issues in 1988

Coupon and conversion premium

The typical coupon and conversion premium of a new Euroconvertible issue vary in accordance with market conditions. As a general guide, premiums on issues from Western companies range anywhere from 10 to 25%, while those from Japanese companies are fixed at around 5% according to Japanese market custom. At the other end of the spectrum, on South Korean issues the premium has been as high as 75 to 125%, reflecting the substantial investor demand for, and scarcity value of, South Korean investments. Coupons are usually fixed somewhere between the borrower's cost of straight debt and the dividend yield on the underlying shares, and are paid annually, except in certain instances where semi-annual coupons are the norm.

Early redemption provisions

At the issuer's option

There are three different types of early redemption, or call, feature usually available to issuers of Euroconvertibles:

1. Provisional call.
2. Absolute call.
3. Tax call.

Most issues have either a non-call period followed by an absolute call, or a provisional call followed by an absolute call. Some convertibles (particularly, for example, Japanese issues) have a combination of all three. Nearly all include a tax call.

1. Provisional call
   A provisional call allows the issuer to call the Euroconvertible for early redemption at any time, but only if the company's share price has appreciated to a pre-determined trigger level. The trigger level is typically 130 to 150% of the initial conversion price, which is usually high enough to provide the convertible investor with a reasonable capital gain and overall return if the bonds are called. The purpose of this call feature is to enable the company to force investors to convert their bonds into equity: usually the call redemption price (i.e. the price the company pays to redeem the convertible) is the par value of the convertible, or a modest premium to it, which is well below the market value of the shares which would be issued upon conversion. As a result, investors faced with a call by the company find it more advantageous to convert into equity rather than surrender to the call. Some issues, particularly those with puts, are provisionally callable from the

outset; in others, there is a period of time, usually three to five years, during which the issue is non-callable, before the provisional call feature operates. A provisional call is potentially disadvantageous to investors because it puts a cap, determined by the trigger level, on the maximum they can make from holding the convertible. Provided the trigger level is high enough, however, this is usually acceptable to most investors.

2. Absolute call

In contrast to most straight (i.e. non-convertible) Eurobonds, most Euroconvertibles are callable at any time under any circumstances from the end of the provisional call or non-call period. Once the provisional or non-call period has expired (typically three to five years from issue date), companies are free to call without pre-condition – an absolute right of call which is unaffected by the company's share price. Of course, except in circumstances where forced conversion is desired, most companies are unlikely to operate the call, because the coupon on the convertible is usually not only lower than that on other forms of borrowing, but also sometimes lower than the cost of paying dividends on the underlying shares. Investors should note, however, that when there is a possibility that the company will call the security, Euroconvertibles whose parity value exceeds the call price will lose their premium in the secondary market, and will trade at parity, or a modest discount to it.

3. Tax call

As with all straight Eurobonds, Euroconvertibles are callable if the tax rules of the issuer's country of origin change so that, for example, withholding tax has to be deducted on all interest payments. (Interest on Euroconvertibles is paid free of any withholding tax.) If it becomes necessary to deduct withholding, and the company is unable to find another method of restructuring the issue to avoid withholding (for example, substituting the borrower with another subsidiary of equal credit standing, but in a tax jurisdiction which permits payments free of withholding tax), then either the bonds can be called or the issuer must increase the coupon so that the next payment to the investor, after deduction of withholding, is the same.

At the investors' option

On non-puttable convertibles, investors have no right of early redemption. They must wait until final maturity after ten or fifteen years to get their money back, if they have not converted the bonds into the underlying shares beforehand. On puttable convertibles, investors have a right to redeem the bonds early, often at a premium to their issue price. Typically this starts after five years. It is either a one-time right exercisable at a specific point, or it is repeated periodically at later dates (e.g. at the end of each year thereafter). Issues with repeated put options are sometimes called rolling or flexible premium put convertibles. Giving the investor the right to redeem early is disadvantageous for the issuer. Compensation usually comes in the form of a much lower coupon and higher conversion premium than is available on a conventional non-puttable security. Repeating the put option in a rolling put convertible lessens the drawbacks for the company even further, because it encourages the investor to hold the security until conversion, rather than redemption, becomes optimal.

Euromarket investors

One of the hallmarks of the Euromarket is anonymity: because all Euroconvertibles are bearer securities, no registers are kept of who the investors are and as a consequence no-one knows for certain the precise breakdown of the Euroconvertible investor base. Only 'guesstimates' provided by market participants are available, and these follow.

Nationality

Exhibit 11.16 estimates the geographic location of the major Euroconvertible investors. In contrast to the straight Eurobond market, where investors are geographically fairly widespread, the majority (approximately 70%) of all Euroconvertibles are purchased by investors located in the United Kingdom and Switzerland. This figure is, however, misleading. For example, almost all the UK investors are not UK investors at all; rather they are foreign investors (e.g. Middle Eastern and Japanese entities) whose funds are managed in London. The same can be said of much of the Swiss investor base, although it is harder to identify who is behind the money managed by the Swiss public and private banks.

114   THE PRINCIPAL MARKETS

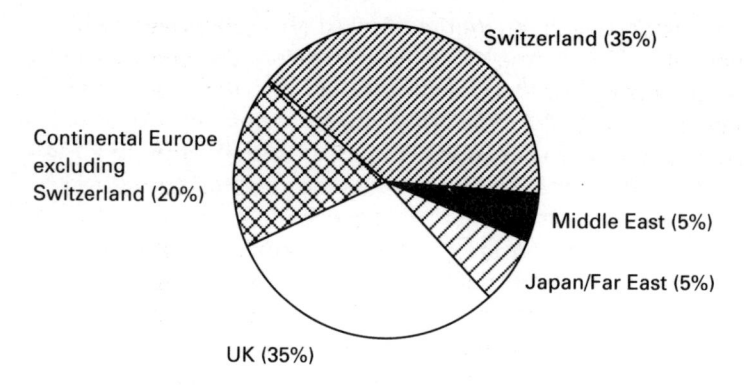

Exhibit 11.16 Euroconvertible market investor profile by physical location of investor

Switzerland (35%)
Continental Europe excluding Switzerland (20%)
Middle East (5%)
Japan/Far East (5%)
UK (35%)

Exhibit 11.17 is another estimate of the investor base in Euroconvertibles, this time obtained by 'looking through' the geographic location of the investor to the real nationality of the funds under management. This reveals a much more geographically diverse pattern of investment, with investors drawn from all over the world, including the Middle East, Switzerland, Japan and the Far East, the United Kingdom, the United States, Scandinavia, and the rest of continental Europe.

Orientation of investor

One of the trends of the 1980s has been the institutionalisation of

Switzerland (30%)
UK (5%)
Benelux (2%)
Germany (3%)
France (5%)
Italy (5%)
Scandinavia (5%)
US (5%)
Other (5%)
Japan/Far East (10%)
Middle East (25%)

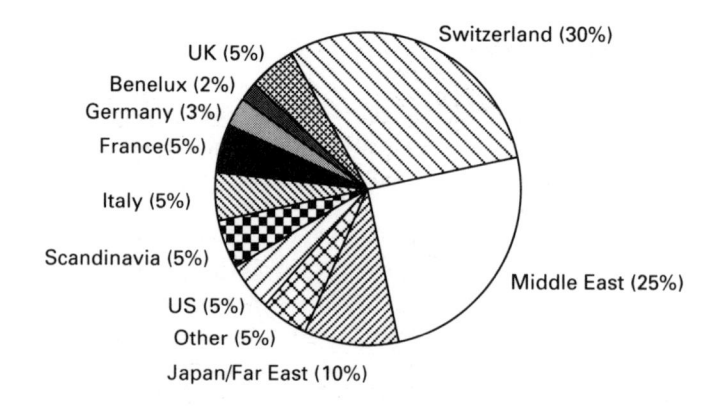

Exhibit 11.17 Euroconvertible market investor profile by nationality of investor

the investor base in the Euromarkets. In the 1960s and to a lesser extent the 1970s, retail investors (private individuals, including the proverbial Belgian dentist) were the predominant buyers of Euroconvertibles. Increasingly, however, it is the institutional investor that now dominates. The Belgian dentist is now more likely to have his money managed for him, rather than investing it directly himself. Exhibit 11.18 illustrates this point by breaking down the investor base into different categories of institutional and retail investors. It can be seen that by far the majority of Euroconvertibles (approximately 85%) are purchased by institutions, ranging from pension funds, money managers and trust banks in the United Kingdom, to insurance companies and private banks in Switzerland.

A significant proportion of institutional investment comes from fixed-income portfolio managers. In this respect, the Euromarket is unique, because in most other major capital markets, convertibles are purchased either by dedicated convertible funds or by equity funds looking to boost yield. Fixed-income (or bond) funds have little or no participation in the convertible market. The opposite is true in the Euromarkets, mainly because of the historical origins of the market. Originally in the 1960s and 1970s, Euroconvertibles were sold to Eurobond investors who were willing to sacrifice a little yield in return for a method, otherwise unavailable, of participating in the bull stock market periods of that era. In the last few years, fixed income convertible investors have been supplanted by dedicated convertible and equity funds, and it is these types of fund which increasingly predominate as the major investors in Euroconvertibles.

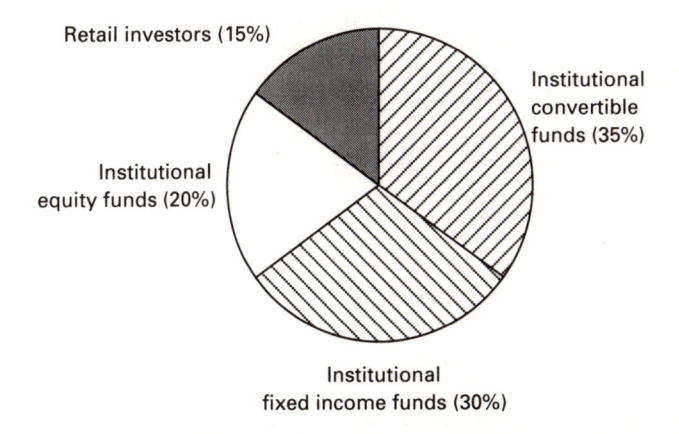

Exhibit 11.18 Euroconvertible market investor profile by type of investor

Regulations governing new issues

In short, there are virtually none. The Euromarket is the world's most freely accessible market and there is no equivalent of the US SEC or Japanese Ministry of Finance to regulate new issue activity. Most issues are listed on the Luxembourg Stock Exchange; however listing requirements are relatively straightforward and can usually be satisfied with disclosure of the type and form customary in the borrower's home market. Most of the policing is undertaken by the lead manager, rather than the exchange, on the basis of what is necessary and prudent in order to market the issue successfully to prospective investors.

Trading and settlement

The Euromarket is centred in London and nearly all the new issue activity, market making and research activities are carried out from there. The liquidity of Euroconvertibles depends both on the size of the issue and on the ability of the market maker to hedge a long convertible position by selling short the underlying shares. US and UK Euroconvertibles are among the most liquid, with those of some Asian borrowers least liquid. Generally, the most liquid of Euroconvertibles can be traded on a 0.75 point spread (i.e. the difference between the market maker's bid and offer should be no more than 0.75% of the convertible's principal amount) for bonds of up to $1 million in face value. Trading is done 'over-the-counter' by telephone. There is as yet no central exchange, and no screens providing live up-to-date prices. Prices quoted do not include accrued interest. This is added to the agreed price and is calculated in the customary Euromarket style, namely on the basis of the number of days elapsed in a year of 360 days comprised of twelve 30 day months. Settlement is usually effected seven calendar days after trade date via one of the two principal clearing houses: Euroclear in Brussels or Cedel in Luxembourg. Physical delivery outside the two clearing houses is possible, although becoming increasingly rare. Book entry within the registers maintained by the clearing houses is usually the norm.

Chapter 12

❖

Overview of the US domestic market

The purpose of this chapter is to provide an overview of the domestic convertible market in the United States: the types of convertible commonly issued, the principal issuers, the major investors, and standard trading and settlement procedures.

The US market is one of the most important convertible markets in the world for both issuers and investors alike. For issuers, it offers access to what is the largest and most sophisticated capital market in the world, as well as extremely attractive terms (conversion premiums are generally higher, and maturities longer, in the US than anywhere else). For investors, it offers a greater degree of choice, higher standards of information disclosure and stock research, and more efficient secondary markets than are available anywhere else in the world. Although issuers up until now have been largely US corporations, the relaxation in the private placement procedures contemplated by the SEC's Rule 144A (adopted in 1990) may open the market up to foreign companies on a much wider scale, which would increase the importance of the US market still further.

Size of market

The US market used to be the world's largest new issue market, but in recent years has been overtaken by Japan and the Euromarket (see Exhibit 12.1). Several factors are responsible for this, including:

1. A diminished need for new equity by US corporations, particularly after the October 1987 crash. This was partly due to reluctance to issue stock at prices which for a long time afterwards were still below those prevailing just prior to the

crash and also due to the increased emphasis being placed in the United States on the use of debt. Many US companies sought to increase, rather than diminish, their leverage, as was illustrated by the extraordinary growth in the junk bond market in the latter half of the 1980s.
2. The regulatory barriers which inhibit non-US companies from accessing the market. SEC registration, as we shall see later, presents a major hurdle to foreign companies wanting to issue in the market, with the consequence that most turn to the Euromarket instead.

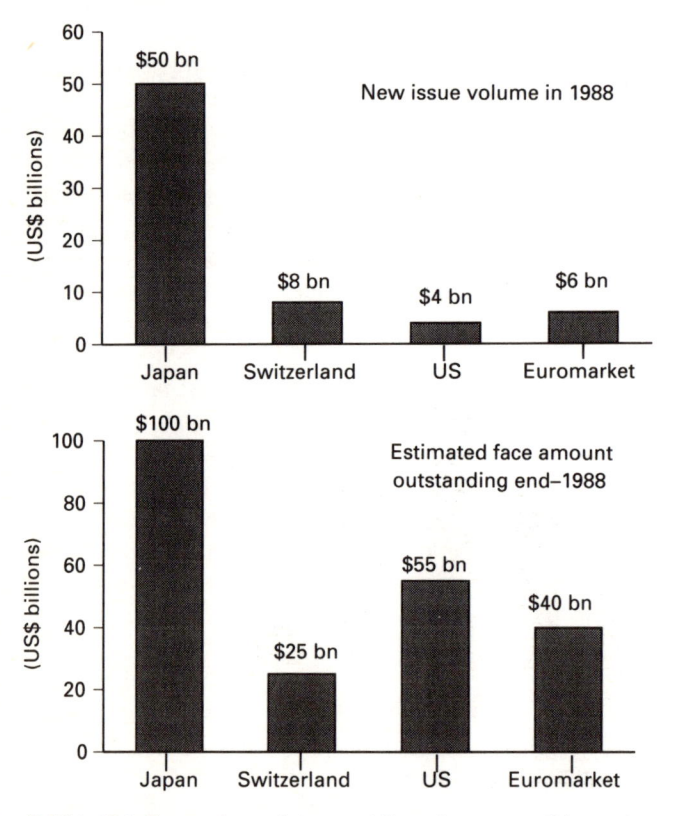

Exhibit 12.1 Comparison of the world's major convertible markets

Exhibit 12.2 shows the pattern of new issue activity in the last few years. It illustrates both an extraordinary surge of activity in the 1985–87 period, followed by an equally remarkable decline in 1988. The decline resulted from US corporations' reluctance to issue equity discussed above. The surge in the 1985–87 period was due to a number of factors including:

1. A strongly rising stock market and falling interest rates, both of which combined to make the terms (i.e. coupon and conversion premium) on new convertible issues particularly attractive to issuers. In the strong bull stock market of the 1986–87 period, investors were prepared to pay higher conversion premiums than normal, while falling interest rates in the same period also enabled coupons to be set at lower than normal levels.
2. A significant increase in the funds available for investing in convertibles, particularly from dedicated convertible funds, i.e. funds established solely to invest convertibles, whose number increased perhaps three or four fold during this period. Part of the increase in dedicated convertible funds was, no doubt, investor response to the surge in new issue activity; a 'chicken and egg' situation in which the growth in new issue activity attracted new investors, which in turn helped encourage favourable new issue conditions. Part of the increase, however, also lies in the increasing complexity of convertible investing, which if to be properly mastered, requires a greater degree of specialised commitment.

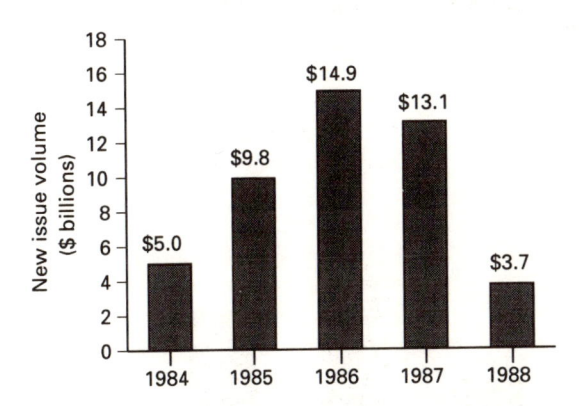

Exhibit 12.2 New issue volume in US convertible market 1984–8 (*Source*: IDD Information Services)

Types of issues

There are four principal types of convertible commonly issued in the US domestic market:

1. Convertible bonds.

2. Convertible preferred.
3. Convertibles with puts.
4. Zero coupon convertibles.

Exhibit 12.3 breaks out 1988's new issue activity by each type of security and, for comparison, issuance of bonds with equity warrants.
Three points are of note:

1. The volume of bonds with equity warrants issuance is particularly low by comparison with the Euromarket. Only $1 billion was issued in the United States compared with $28 billion in the Euromarket in the same period. This is partly due to the inability of certain US investors to purchase warrants (warrants are deemed to be 'wasting assets', which certain institutions are prohibited by charter from investing in) and partly to a reluctance on the part of US companies to issue warrants. Equity warrants are perceivd by many in the United States to be issued primarily by lower credit quality companies, and then only to enhance the attractiveness of an otherwise unsellable debt issue.
2. There is a flourishing convertible preferred market, similar to that prevailing in the UK domestic market. No other market offers preferred issues of such size and variety.

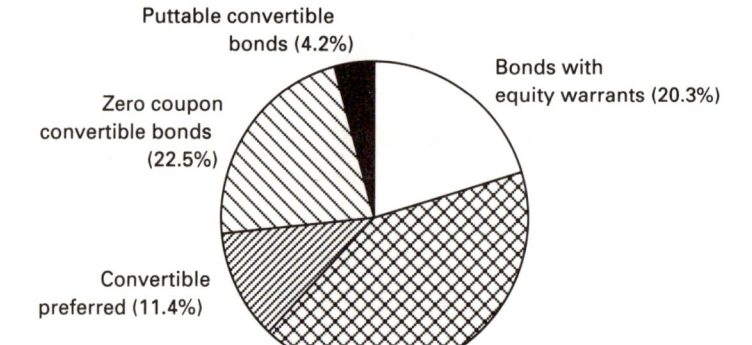

Total: US$ 4.6 billion

- Puttable convertible bonds (4.2%)
- Zero coupon convertible bonds (22.5%)
- Convertible preferred (11.4%)
- Bonds with equity warrants (20.3%)
- Conventional convertible bonds (41.7%)

Exhibit 12.3 Hybrid securities offered in the US convertible market in 1988 (*Source*: IDD Information Services)

3. There was an active market in 1988 for zero coupon convertibles. Investor interest in these instruments has fluctuated widely: first introduced in 1985, there were only two issues in 1986 and none in 1987. Since this is an instrument whose risk/reward characteristics tend to favour the issuer rather than the investor, this pattern is not surprising. The decline in zero coupon convertible issuance during what was otherwise a boom period for convertibles is attributable to investor resistance to the security: when there were plenty of other types of convertible to invest in, investors had no need to purchase zeros. Equally, the increase in 1988 activity can be attributed to the extreme shortage of other types of convertible; with little other choice, dedicated convertible buyers were more willing to purchase zeros.

Types of issuer

Exhibit 12.4 breaks out the volume of convertibles outstanding at the end of 1988 by industrial classification of the issuer. One of the most attractive features of the US convertible market from the investors' perspective is the wide variety of issues offered; almost every sector of the US economy is represented, and within each sector there are usually plenty of issues to choose from. Only the Japanese market comes close in providing investors with such a variety of investment choice.

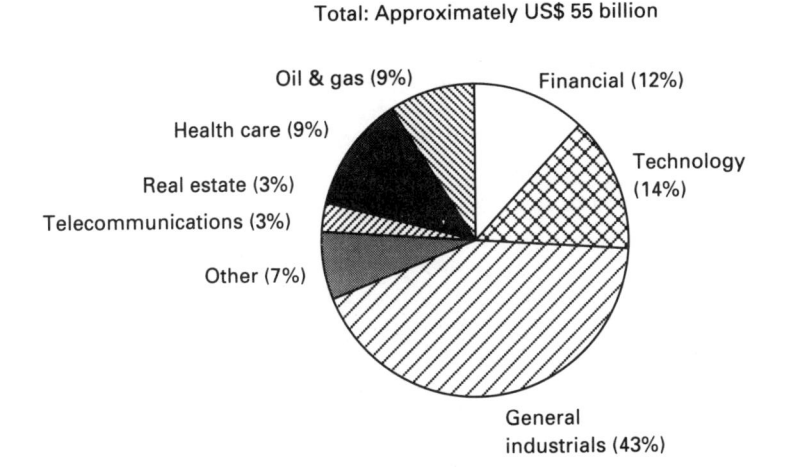

Total: Approximately US$ 55 billion

Oil & gas (9%)
Financial (12%)
Health care (9%)
Technology (14%)
Real estate (3%)
Telecommunications (3%)
Other (7%)
General industrials (43%)

Exhibit 12.4 Face amount outstanding by industry group in the US convertible market at the end of 1988

THE PRINCIPAL MARKETS

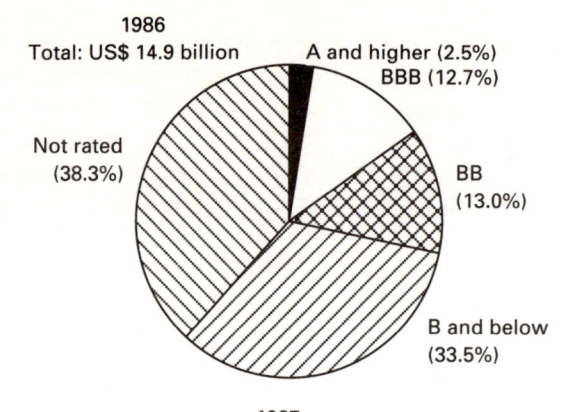

1986
Total: US$ 14.9 billion

- A and higher (2.5%)
- BBB (12.7%)
- BB (13.0%)
- B and below (33.5%)
- Not rated (38.3%)

1987
Total: US$ 13.1 billion

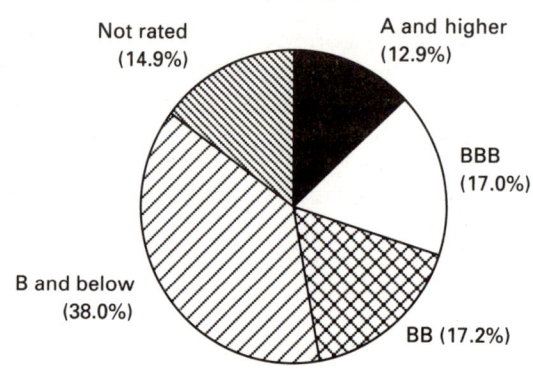

- A and higher (12.9%)
- BBB (17.0%)
- BB (17.2%)
- B and below (38.0%)
- Not rated (14.9%)

1988
Total: US$ 3.7 billion

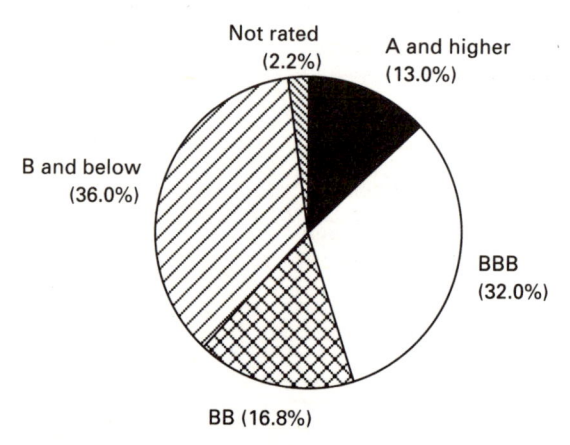

- A and higher (13.0%)
- BBB (32.0%)
- BB (16.8%)
- B and below (36.0%)
- Not rated (2.2%)

Exhibit 12.5 New issue volume analysed by credit rating in the US convertible market 1986–8 (*Source*: IDD Information Services)

Credit quality

Exhibit 12.5 illustrates the breakdown of new issue volume from 1986 to 1988 by credit quality of the issuer. One possible drawback of the US market from the investors' perspective is illustrated here: the under-representation of high credit quality issues relative to the situation in the stock and bond markets. Low credit quality companies tend to make more use of convertibles in the United States than do their high credit quality counterparts. This is the opposite to the situation prevailing in Japan, where most of Japan's blue-chip companies have issued convertibles at one time or another.

Exhibit 12.5 also illustrates another by-product of the October 1987 crash – the so-called 'flight to quality'. Investment grade issues (those rated BBB or better) comprised only 15.2% of 1986 new issue volume, but rose to 45.1% in 1988. Correspondingly, unrated issues (generally those from companies with the lowest credit quality) decreased from 38.3% of total issue volume in 1986 to 2.2% in 1988. In the October 1987 crash, the higher credit quality issues were among the most liquid and best performing (i.e. declined in value the least), with the result that investors showed a marked preference for such issues in the period afterwards.

Largest issues

A list of the largest ever convertible issues in the US domestic

Date	Company	Amount raised
Jan. 1990	Time Warner	$5,300m
Sep. 1986	Unisys	$1,425m
Nov. 1984	IBM	$1,285m
Jun. 1990	Walt Disney (exchangeable into Euro Disney)	$ 927m
Nov. 1985	Baxter Travenol	$ 541m
Aug. 1986	Warner Communications	$ 500m
Sep. 1988	Amoco	$ 498m
Oct. 1989	Loews	$ 443m
Mar. 1983	MCI Communications	$ 435m
Jun. 1990	Du Pont	$ 404m
Mar. 1980	Digital Equipment	$ 400m
Sep. 1984	Digital Equipment	$ 400m
Oct. 1988	Waste Management	$ 400m
Sep. 1989	Berkshire Hathaway	$ 400m

Exhibit 12.6 The largest issues in the US convertible market

market is presented in Exhibit 12.6. The largest ever issue, a $5.3 billion convertible preferred offering resulting from the merger of Time and Warner Communications in 1989 is notable because it is substantially bigger than its equivalent in the other major convertible markets.

Foreign issuers

The number of non-US companies accessing the US market has been very limited, as Exhibit 12.7 illustrates. The major factor inhibiting foreign issuance has been the considerable regulatory burden associated with a public offering in the United States. All public issues are regulated by the SEC which requires all potential foreign issuers to reconcile locally prepared financial statements to accounting standards prevailing in the United States and to provide disclosure on business activities which usually exceeds that of home country practices. This has proved too cumbersome for most foreign companies, with the result that nearly all turn to the Swiss market or Euromarket instead.

A secondary factor which has also inhibited foreign convertible offerings has been the lack of a liquid market in the United States for the underlying equity. This deters some US convertible investors from purchasing foreign convertibles. Even though

Date	Company	Nationality	Amount raised
Jun. 1978	Ito-Yokado	Japan	$ 50m
Aug. 1979	Canon	Japan	$ 80m
Jul. 1980	Ricoh	Japan	$ 60m
Nov. 1980	American Israeli Paper Mills	Israel	$ 11m
Mar. 1981	Elron Electronic Industries	Israel	$ 10m
Apr. 1981	Hitachi	Japan	$150m
Jul. 1981	Ito-Yokado	Japan	$ 60m
Aug. 1984	Makita Electric Works	Japan	$ 50m
Jul. 1985	NBS Capital	Canada	$ 20m
May 1986	Sea Containers	Bermuda	$ 75m
Sep. 1986	Laser Industries	Israel	$ 20m
May 1987	Kinburn Technology	Canada	$ 90m
Jun. 1987	Varity	Canada	$116m
Jun. 1989	Biogen	Switzerland	$ 60m
Feb. 1989	Newscorp (exchangeable into Reuters)	Australia/UK	$ 94m
Nov. 1989	Millicom (exchangeable into Racal)	US/UK	$ 60m

Exhibit 12.7 Foreign issuers in the US convertible market

there may be a liquid market for the issuer's stock in its home country, most US investors do not have direct access to foreign stock markets for information on share prices (having to rely instead on brokers), with the result that they find it difficult to value and trade the associated convertible.

The SEC has recently introduced a new set of regulations (Rule 144A) which may, over time, help change this picture. The purpose of Rule 144A includes making it easier for foreign companies to launch private placements in the United States to 'qualified' institutional investors (broadly speaking, most of the major institutions), on the basis of disclosure and financial reporting standards acceptable in the home market, rather than those required for US public offerings. If the Rule 144A private placement market develops as envisaged, then it may result in foreign issuers being able to launch convertibles in the US market much more frequently than has hitherto been possible.

Since funds available for investment in the United States are increasingly controlled by institutions (see Exhibits 12.8 and 12.9), and US investor interest in foreign stocks is increasing (see Exhibit 12.10), the prospects for increased convertible issuance from foreign companies in the future look promising, even if it takes time to develop.

Households: aggregate ten year sales of $625 billion
Institutions: aggregate ten year purchases of $305 billion

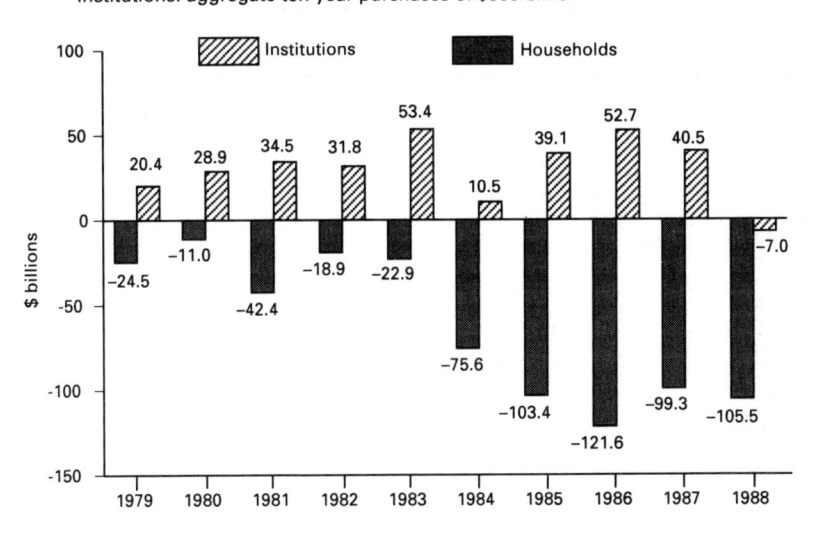

Exhibit 12.8 Net acquisitions/sales of corporate equities by households and institutions (*Source*: Federal Reserve, *Flow of Funds Quarterly Report*)

1981
Total: US$ 1,497 billion

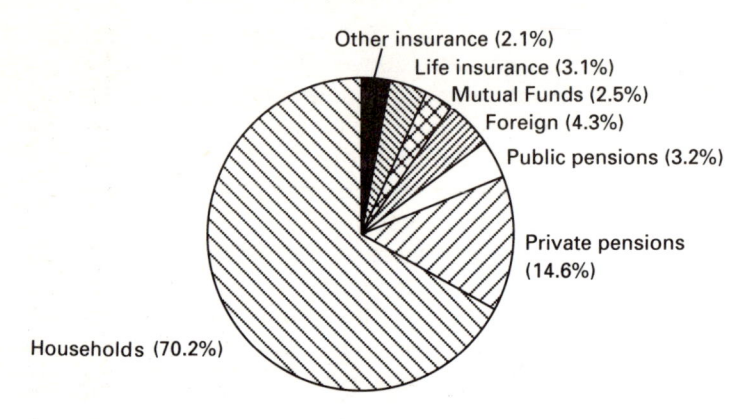

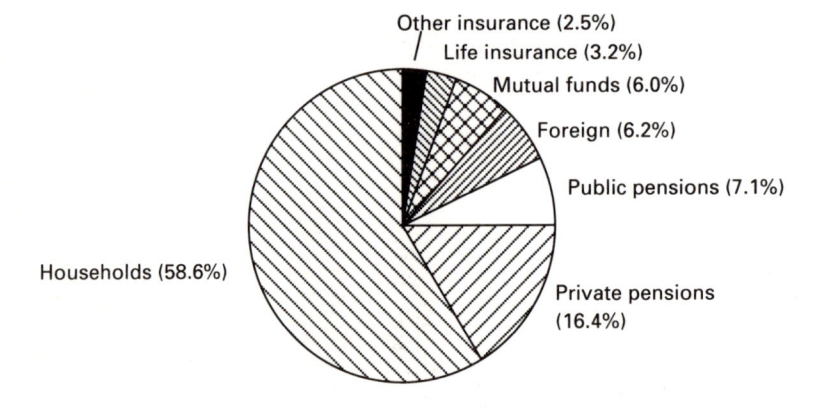

- Other insurance (2.1%)
- Life insurance (3.1%)
- Mutual Funds (2.5%)
- Foreign (4.3%)
- Public pensions (3.2%)
- Private pensions (14.6%)
- Households (70.2%)

- Other insurance (2.5%)
- Life insurance (3.2%)
- Mutual funds (6.0%)
- Foreign (6.2%)
- Public pensions (7.1%)
- Private pensions (16.4%)
- Households (58.6%)

Exhibit 12.9 Breakdown of US equity holdings in 1981 and 1988 (*Source*: Federal Reserve, *Flow of Funds Quarterly Report*)

Typical convertible issue

Average size

The size of the average convertible offering is approximately $70 million, as Exhibit 12.11 illustrates. It also shows that there has been a marked increase in the average size in the last few years. Part of this is attributable to the effects of the October 1987 crash. The larger issues were more liquid during the crash (i.e.

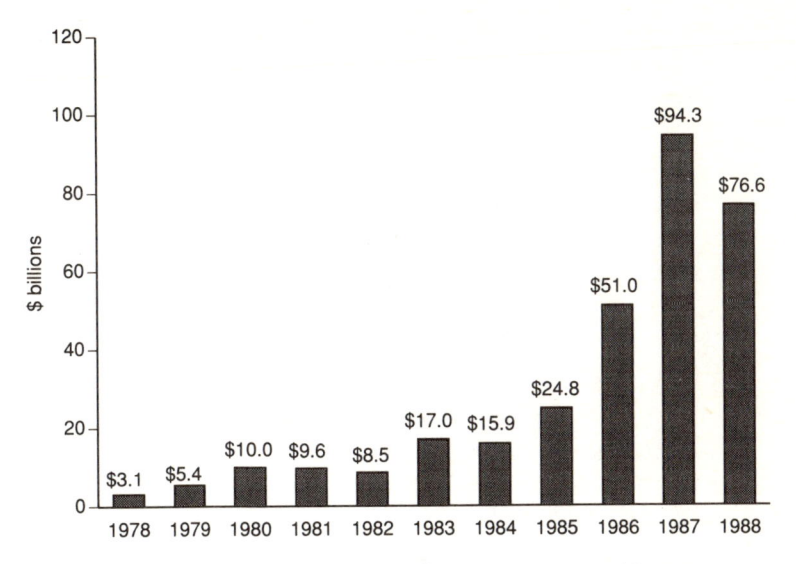

Exhibit 12.10 Gross US purchases of foreign stock 1978–88 (*Source: US Treasury Bulletin,* June 1989)

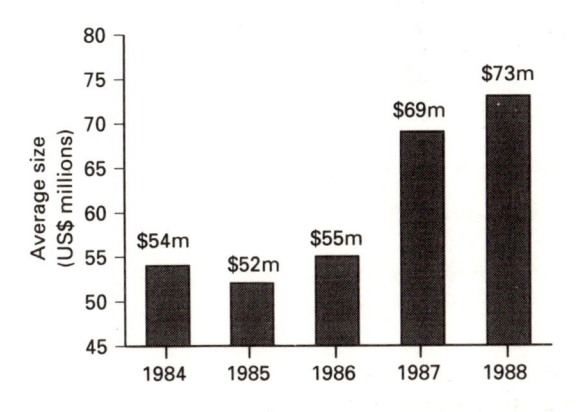

Exhibit 12.11 Average size of convertible issues in the US market 1984–8

investors found them easier to trade) with the result that investors have shown a marked preference for larger-sized offerings since.

Maturity

Exhibit 12.12 shows that with the exception of convertible preferred offerings, which have no final redemption date, most

128   THE PRINCIPAL MARKETS

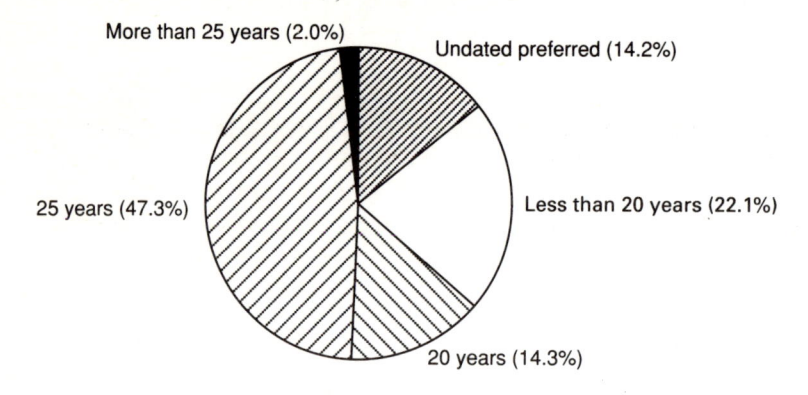

Exhibit 12.12 New issue volume analysed by final maturity in the US convertible market in 1988

Total: US$ 3.7 billion

- More than 25 years (2.0%)
- Undated preferred (14.2%)
- 25 years (47.3%)
- Less than 20 years (22.1%)
- 20 years (14.3%)

offerings in the US have a final maturity of twenty or twenty five years. Including convertible preferred issues, nearly 80% of 1988's new issues had a final maturity of twenty years or longer. This makes the US market particularly attractive for issuers, because no other market offers such long maturities so consistently.

Coupon and conversion premium

For most conventional convertible offerings the conversion premium is typically between 20 and 30%, and the coupon is established at a point between the dividend yield on the stock and the coupon required for a straight bond offering, to give a breakeven to the investor of between three and five years. The exceptions to this are primarily zero coupon convertibles, where the investor forgoes coupon income in return for a lower initial conversion premium (typically in the 12–18% range) and the right to redeem the bonds early at a premium to their issue price. The investor's yield to put or redemption on a zero coupon convertible is usually roughly the same as the coupon that would otherwise have been paid on a conventional convertible. Coupons in the United States are typically paid semi-annually. There is no withholding tax deducted if the investor identifies himself and his US taxpayer ID number to the borrower. Failure to do so results in part of the coupon being withheld by the borrower.

Early redemption features

Mandatory redemption

Most conventional convertible bonds operate a sinking fund, usually starting after ten years, designed to retire approximately 70–80% of the issue prior to final maturity. The resulting average life is approximately sixteen to twenty years. There are no sinking funds in zero coupon convertibles or convertible preferreds.

Issuer's optional redemption

Convertible bonds or preferred are typically callable for early redemption by the issuer after three to five years under any circumstance – an absolute right of call which Euroconvertibles also incorporate. There is usually a small, declining, premium over the par value of the security which the issuer must pay to operate the call.

Convertibles are also often provisionally callable, i.e. callable in the first three to five years as well, but only in circumstances where the underlying share price has appreciated to the point where an investor converting the security into its underlying shares would benefit from a significant capital gain. Usually the share price trigger level at which this call feature can be operated is set at 150% of the conversion price, although it is sometimes reduced to as low as 130%. Zero coupon convertibles have similar call features, although the trigger levels and the redemption prices are adjusted upwards to reflect the accretion in the value of the bonds.

Investor's optional redemption

Unlike the Euromarket, puttable convertibles are relatively uncommon in the US (only 4.2% of 1988's new issue volume were puttable convertibles – see Exhibit 12.3), being offered generally by lower credit quality borrowers and only when the omission of a put would make the convertible otherwise unsellable. There is one exception to this: zero coupon convertibles. Nearly all zero coupon convertibles enable the investor to put the bonds back to the issuer at their accreted value at several points during the life of the security, usually starting after three to five years.

Investors

Exhibits 12.8 and 12.9 have shown how increasingly institutional the US market is becoming. It is also becoming highly specialised, as is evidenced by the fact that the majority of US convertible investors are dedicated convertible buyers, i.e. institutional funds whose sole mandate is to invest in convertibles. No other market is quite like this; in most of the other major convertible markets, convertible investing is treated as a sideline to stock or bond investing, i.e. convertibles are purchased as part of an overall stock or bond portfolio. In this respect, therefore, US convertible investors are among the most sophisticated of the world's convertible buyers.

Exhibit 12.13 illustrates the specialisation of the US market by providing the typical breakdown of investors in a new US convertible issue. More than 50% is purchased by dedicated convertible funds, with the second largest component being purchased by equity investors.

Exhibit 12.9 provides an overview of US institutional and retail investment in equities. It can be seen that by far the dominant institutional buyers are US pension funds, who make investments either directly, or via outside fund managers. A similar situation prevails in the convertible market.

Trading and settlement

Most large size convertible bonds are quoted on a 0.75 point

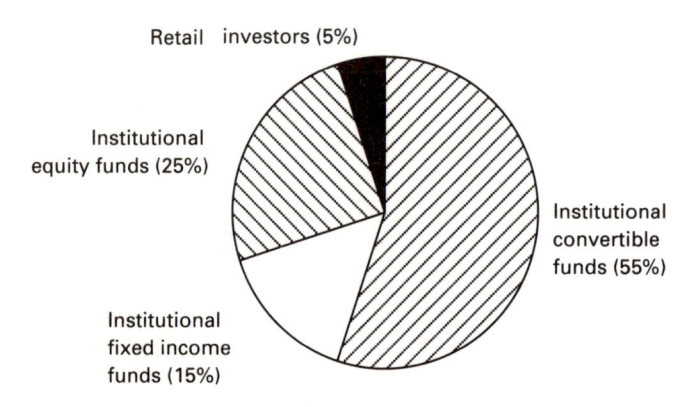

Exhibit 12.13 Investor profile of a typical new issue in the US convertible market

spread, for dealing in sizes of up to $1 million. Trading in most issues is over-the-counter, i.e. by telephone, although for exchange listed securities, there is a 'tape' which provides price data real-time. The quoted price does not include accrued interest, which is added to the purchaser's costs. Interest is calculated on the basis of the number of days elapsed in a year of 360 days. Settlement is due five business days after trade date and is effected by book entry through the principal securities clearing house in the United States, Depository Trust Company. Physical settlement is rare and cumbersome. On some issues it is impossible: definitive bonds are never printed and the issue exists only in book form at Depository Trust Company.

Chapter 13

❖

Overview of the Swiss market

The purpose of this chapter is to provide an overview of the convertible market in Switzerland, particularly for non-Swiss issuers and investors. It reviews the principal types of convertible in use, typical terms, typical issuers and, to the extent that it is possible to identify them, typical investors.

The Swiss market is important for issuers and investors in at least two respects. Firstly, after the Japanese domestic market, it is the world's second largest in terms of recent new issue activity (see Exhibit 13.1). Secondly, it is an extraordinarily international market: more than 90% of new issue activity in Switzerland comes from non-Swiss companies (see Exhibit 13.2). This is the exact opposite of all other domestic markets worldwide, where nearly all new issues are from domestic issuers. Swiss investors have had a longer tradition of international investing than investors in almost any other country, and this is reflected in the new issue activity for non-Swiss issuers.

Size of market

The growth of new issue activity over the years in the Swiss market is illustrated in Exhibit 13.3. At first glance the statistics seem to reveal a decline in activity in the boom period for other convertible markets of 1984 to 1986. This observation is misleading, however. By far the bulk of new Swiss franc convertibles during the 1984 to 1988 period were from Japanese corporations and banks (see Exhibit 13.2) and the apparent decline in Swiss new issue activity is solely attributable to a decline in Japanese issuance. This in turn was due to the boom in the Japanese domestic convertible market which happened at about the same time. Japanese companies which up until that point had issued in the Swiss convertible market turned instead to the domestic

New issue volume in 1988

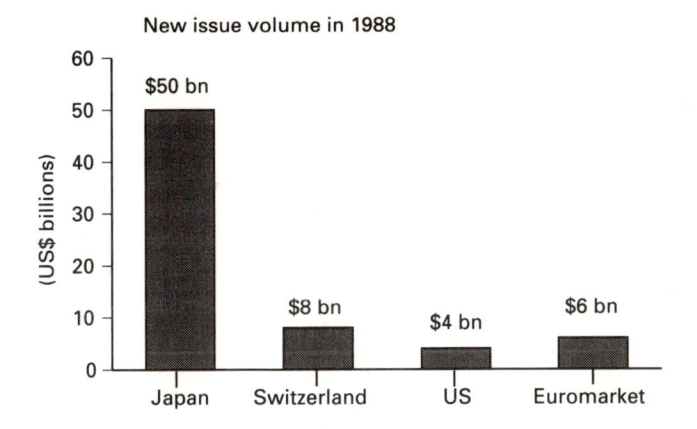

- Japan: $50 bn
- Switzerland: $8 bn
- US: $4 bn
- Euromarket: $6 bn

Estimated face amount outstanding end-1988

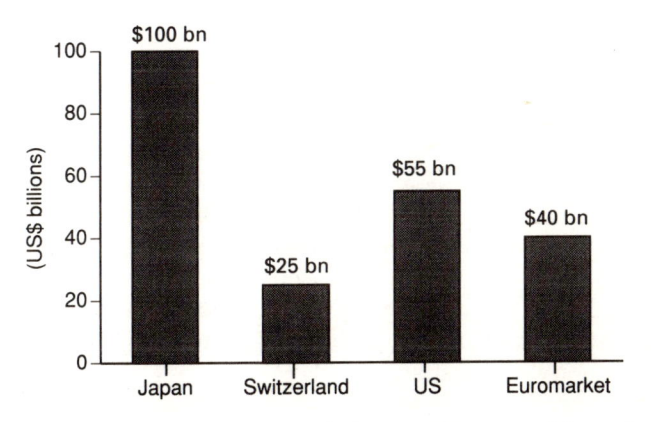

- Japan: $100 bn
- Switzerland: $25 bn
- US: $55 bn
- Euromarket: $40 bn

Exhibit 13.1 **Comparison of the world's major convertible markets**

market in Japan, where strong investor demand, longer maturities and the absence of currency risk fuelled strong new issue conditions. When Japanese new issue activity is stripped out of Exhibit 13.3, the pattern of new issue activity in Switzerland is similar to that of other major convertible markets: relatively strong growth prior to 1987, then a temporary lull in the aftermath of October 1987, followed by a resumption of growth in 1988.

Types of issue

There are two principal types of convertible issue in the Swiss market:

1986
Volume: SF 4.3 billion

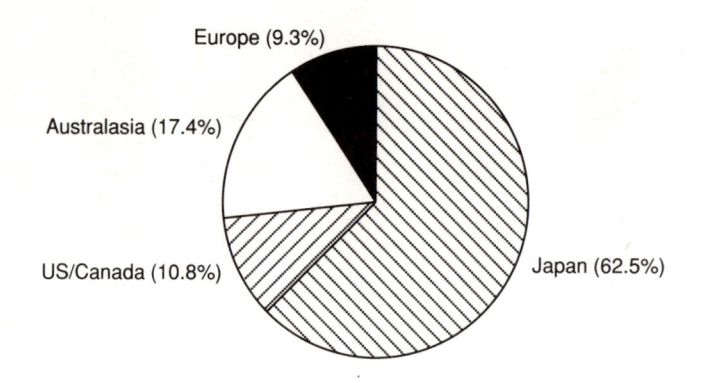

- Europe (9.3%)
- Australasia (17.4%)
- US/Canada (10.8%)
- Japan (62.5%)

1987
Volume: SF 6.8 billion

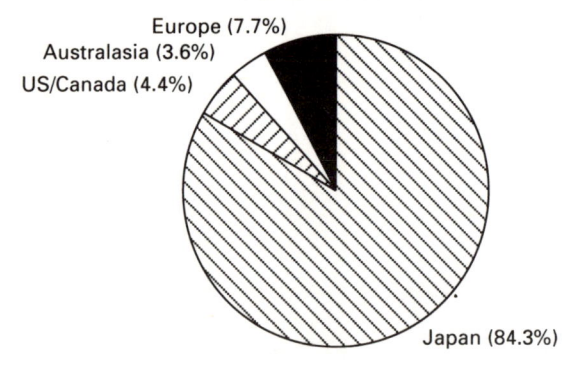

- Europe (7.7%)
- Australasia (3.6%)
- US/Canada (4.4%)
- Japan (84.3%)

1988
Volume SF 11.2 billion

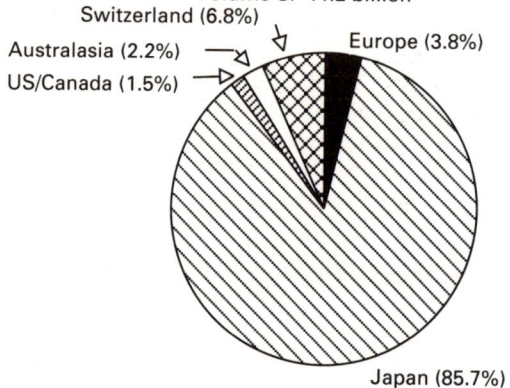

- Switzerland (6.8%)
- Europe (3.8%)
- Australasia (2.2%)
- US/Canada (1.5%)
- Japan (85.7%)

Exhibit 13.2 Issue volume analysed by nationality in the Swiss convertible market 1986–8 (*Source*: Euromoney Swissware)

OVERVIEW OF THE SWISS MARKET 135

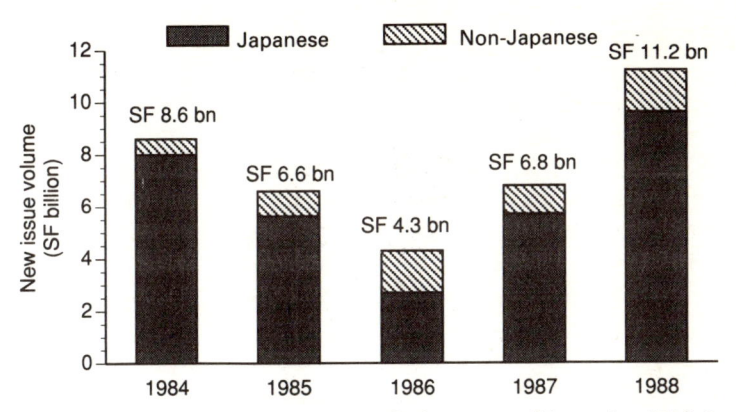

Exhibit 13.3 New issue volume in the Swiss convertible market 1984–8 (*Source*: Euromoney Swissware)

1. Conventional convertibles.
2. Premium put convertibles.

New issue activity in 1988 for each type of security and, for comparison, bond with equity warrants is illustrated in Exhibit 13.4.

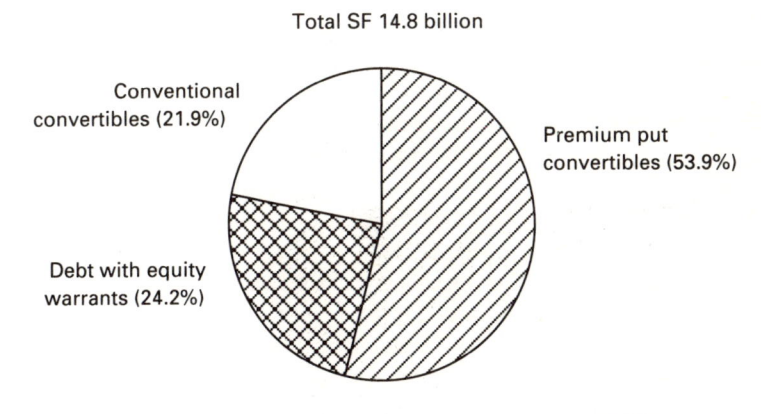

Exhibit 13.4 Hybrid equity issues in the Swiss market in 1988 (*Source*: Euromoney Swissware)

The Swiss market is relatively unique in that there is a flourishing bonds with equity warrants sector alongside the convertible market. Only the Euromarket has a similar pattern of activity. By contrast, bonds with equity warrants issuance in the Japanese or US markets has been relatively insignificant. There are several reasons for the high level of activity in Switzerland.

First, the premium available on a Swiss franc bonds with equity warrants issue is often higher than that on a convertible, enabling issuing companies to sell shares at a higher price than is possible on a convertible. The Swiss market is unique in this respect: in most other markets, particularly for example the Euromarket, investors significantly undervalue warrants, often paying no more than one-half to two-thirds their theoretical value. A second reason favouring a bonds with warrants issue is that the financing is slightly more tax efficient for the issuer. The proceeds of the issue can, in certain circumstances, be split in two, with part attributable to the issue of the warrants and part to the issue of the bonds. The bonds are thereby effectively issued at a discount, and the discount can be amortised for tax purposes as well as the coupon. In contrast only the coupon on a convertible can be deducted for the tax purposes. While the tax efficiency of a bonds with warrants issue is available to issuers in other markets, the advantage is often lost by the lower warrant premium so that the convertible remains the more attractive alternative overall.

A third factor underlying the relatively high issuance of Swiss franc bonds with warrants is the availability of currency swaps to hedge the foreign exchange risks of the bond portion. Swiss franc convertibles cannot be hedged; as a consequence, given the generally appreciating trend of the Swiss franc against most other currencies, foreign companies wanting to access the Swiss market are much less willing to issue a convertible than a bonds with warrants issue. A currency swap can hedge the foreign exchange risks of a Swiss franc bonds with warrants issue because it provides the issuer with the Swiss francs required to pay the coupon and principal on the bonds, in return for similar payments from the issuer denominated in the issuer's home currency. There is no foreign exchange risk on the warrant portion, because it is customary in the Swiss market to denominate the exercise price of the warrants in the issuer's home currency, rather than Swiss francs. As a result, the foreign exchange risks of a bonds with warrants issue can be completely eliminated.

In contrast, the foreign exchange risks of a convertible cannot be hedged because the conversion date is not known in advance for certain. If a convertible were swapped and conversion were to take place before the swap matures, the issuer would be left with a significant foreign exchange exposure from the swap, with no offsetting liability from the convertible. Notwithstanding this, many Japanese companies, and some non-Japanese companies, still choose to issue Swiss franc convertibles because Swiss franc convertibles offer one feature not offered by bonds with warrants issues: a higher probability of early conversion. Either as a result of investor preference, or as a result of the issuer forcing the investor to do so by calling the bonds, convertibles are often converted into equity well before final maturity. In contrast, warrants are exercised prior to final maturity much less frequently and there is no right of call for the issuer.

New issue activity in Swiss franc premium put convertibles is determined primarily by investor sentiment towards the underlying equity. All other things being equal, issuers prefer not to offer puts, on the basis that they increase the risk of early redemption and lessen the chances of conversion into equity. Investors, on the other hand, may require them, particularly in periods where sentiment about the future strength of the share price is not particularly bullish. This is illustrated by new issue activity in premium put convertibles in 1987 and 1988. In the first nine months of 1987, before the October crash, investor sentiment was particularly bullish, with the result that less than 15% of new issues had to be offered with puts. In contrast, in 1988, the after effects of the crash were still being felt, with the result that more than 70% of new issues had to incorporate puts.

Nationality of issues

Exhibit 13.2 illustrates the breakdown of new issue volume in the last three years by nationality of issuer. The preponderance of Japanese companies and, equally, the relative absence of Swiss issuers, is remarkable by contrast to other major convertible markets. One reason why Japanese companies have been and may continue to be the predominant foreign issuers of Swiss franc convertibles is the strength of the yen. Because the foreign exchange risk on a Swiss franc convertible is not hedgeable, non-Japanese companies have been reluctant to issue in Swiss francs. Only Japanese companies, with the benefit of a strong yen as their home currency, have generally been willing to assume this risk.

The reluctance of non-Japanese companies to issue Swiss franc convertibles has in some cases also been matched by a decline in investor demand. For example, the significant decline in

North American new issue activity over the 1986–88 period coincided with the substantial decline in the US dollar on the foreign exchange market over the same period. For Swiss investors, the growth in the US stock market was often more than offset by the decline in the US dollar, rendering Swiss franc convertibles from US issuers relatively unattractive investments when performance was measured in Swiss franc terms. The apparent absence of Swiss issuers from their home market is attributable to a number of factors, including:

1. A relative paucity (by comparison with other countries) of Swiss companies of a size and stature capable of launching public offerings.
2. A flourishing bonds with warrants sector. As previously mentioned, a bonds with warrants issue in Switzerland often provides issuers with a higher premium than a convertible, and is more tax efficient, with the result that many Swiss companies opt for a bonds with warrants issue instead.
3. The relatively less attractive performance of the Swiss stock market over this period (while the market advanced the gains were not as substantial as those of, for example, the Japanese market, even after adjusting for currency movements), making Swiss equity-linked issues less attractive to investors than Japanese issues.
4. A withholding tax of 30% on all interest coupons paid by Swiss borrowers. No withholding tax is levied on foreign convertibles, with the result that these are relatively more attractive to investors from a yield perspective.

Exhibits 13.5 to 13.8 give selected examples of recent Swiss franc convertibles from Swiss, European, US, Australasian and Japanese borrowers.

Largest and smallest issues

These are listed in Exhibits 13.9 and 13.10. While the largest issues are comparable in size to the largest issues in most other major convertible markets, the Swiss market is unique in offering very small scale financings which would be all but impossible in other markets. For example, the smallest issue since 1980, for which details are publicly available, is a SF 6 million (approxi-

Date	Issuer	Nationality	Amount
Feb. 1986	Aegon	Netherlands	SF300m
Jan. 1987	Dumenil Leble	France	SF100m
Feb. 1987	Mountleigh	UK	SF125m
May 1987	Polly Peck	UK	SF 65m
May 1987	LM Ericsson	Sweden	SF135m
Apr. 1988	Michelin	France	SF125m
May 1988	Remy et Associes	France	SF175m
Jul. 1988	Julius Baer	Switzerland	SF150m
Jul. 1988	Ciba Geigy	Switzerland	SF150m
Jul. 1988	EMS Chemie Holding	Switzerland	SF160m

Exhibit 13.5 Selected Swiss and European issuers in the Swiss convertible market 1984–8

Date	Issuer	Amount
Aug. 1984	Wang Labs	SF200m
Sep. 1984	Pan Am	SF100m
Dec. 1984	Gillette	SF160m
Feb. 1985	Wang Labs	SF200m
Jun. 1985	Pan Am	SF100m
Nov. 1985	LSI Logic	SF 40m
Dec. 1985	Peoples Express	SF150m
Dec. 1986	Peoples Express	SF150m
Dec. 1986	Bio Capital Holding	SF100m
Oct. 1988	American Health Properties	SF 35m

Exhibit 13.6 Selected US issuers in the Swiss convertible market 1984–8

Date	Issuer	Nationality	Amount
Nov. 1985	Chase Corp.	New Zealand	SF145m
Feb. 1986	Brierley Investments	New Zealand	SF100m
Jun. 1986	Shield Enterprises	Australia	SF200m
Oct. 1986	Elders IXL	Australia	SF200m
Oct. 1986	Bell Resources	Australia	SF250m
Jan. 1987	Elders IXL	Australia	SF125m
Oct. 1987	Carter Holt Harvey	New Zealand	SF100m
Feb. 1988	Newscorp (exchangeable into Pearson)	Australia	SF150m
Sep. 1988	Bond International Gold	Australia	SF100m

Exhibit 13.7 Selected Australasian issuers in the Swiss convertible market 1984–8

Date	Issuer	Amount
Jun. 1984	Sharp	SF300m
Jun. 1985	Fujitsu	SF250m
Oct. 1985	Sanyo Electric	SF250m
Jun. 1980	C Itoh	SF300m
Jul. 1988	Atsugi Nylon	SF250m
Aug. 1988	Tobishima Corp	SF300m
Mar. 1989	Mitsubishi Oil	SF300m
Jun. 1989	Sumitomo Electric	SF300m
Jul. 1989	Nisshin Steel	SF300m
Oct. 1989	Rohm	SF300m

Exhibit 13.8 Selected Japanese issuers in the Swiss convertible market 1984–8

Date	Issuer	Nationality	Amount
May 1989	Dai Ichi Kangyo Bank	Japan	SF1,000m*
Apr. 1989	Fuji Bank	Japan	SF 800m*
Jan. 1989	Sumitomo Bank	Japan	SF 700m*
May 1989	Tobishima Corp.	Japan	SF 500m
Mar. 1989	Nomura Securities	Japan	SF 500m*
Feb. 1989	Bank of Tokyo	Japan	SF 500m*
May 1986	Sumitomo Realty & Development	Japan	SF 500m
Jul. 1989	Atsugi Nylon	Japan	SF 400m
Jul. 1989	Sumitomo Trust	Japan	SF 350m
Nov. 1985	Sumitomo Realty	Japan	SF 350m

Note: *Multi-tranche offerings

Exhibit 13.9 The largest issues in the Swiss convertible market

Date	Issuer	Nationality	Amount
Nov. 1988	Personal Computer Products	US	SF 6m
Nov. 1988	Aroser Verkehrsbetriebe	Switzerland	SF10m
Jul. 1984	Biosearch Medical Products	US	SF10m
Aug. 1987	Horizon Gold Shares	US	SF12m
Jan. 1984	Choguku Marine Paints	Japan	SF15m
Jul. 1985	Hokkai Can	Japan	SF15m
Mar. 1988	Fuchs Petrolub	Switzerland	SF17m
Oct. 1989	Nippon Pillar Packaging	Japan	SF18m
Sep. 1989	Northern Feather	Denmark	SF18m

Exhibit 13.10 The smallest issues in the Swiss convertible market

mately $3.5 million) issue for Personal Computer Products of the United States. The total size of the issue is not much more than the up-front costs (underwriting commissions, lawyers' and accountants' fees, printing expenses etc.) of a public offering in the United States!

One of the main reasons why smaller issues are possible in Switzerland is that secondary market liquidity is less important to Swiss investors than investors elsewhere. Perhaps more than anywhere else in the world, Swiss investors have a reputation for long-term investment, and exhibit much less of the trading mentality that has increasingly dominated institutional investment elsewhere in the world. As a consequence, smaller issues, which by their size are less easy to trade than larger transactions, are more feasible in the Swiss market.

Typical convertible issue

Size

As if to emphasise the point that smaller issues are more feasible in the Swiss market, the average size of a Swiss convertible was only approximately SF 80 million ($ 50 million) in 1988 (see Exhibit 13.11). In most other markets, this would be considered a little on the small side to create the best secondary market liquidity, so that a premium would have to be paid by the issuer. This is not the case in Switzerland, where smaller issues are more acceptable and there is little, if any, premium paid for liquidity.

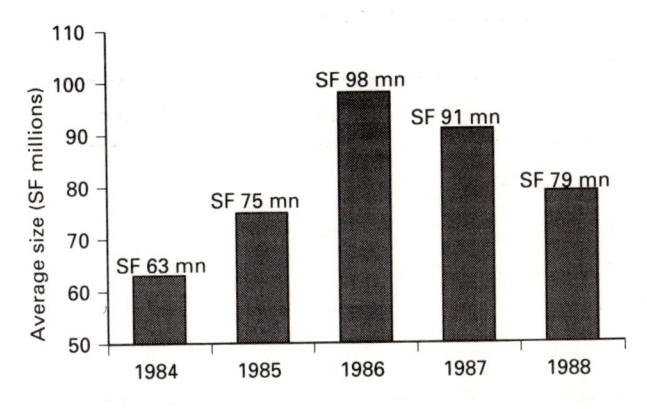

Exhibit 13.11 Average size of issues in the Swiss convertible market 1984–8

Maturity

The Swiss market is predominantly short term (see Exhibit 13.12). This can be a drawback for issuers using a convertible as a method of raising long-term capital, but a bonus for investors seeking convertibles with above average downside protection. In 1988, for example, more than 80% of new issues had a maturity of five years or less. Only 5% had a maturity of longer than seven years. No other convertible market in the world offers such a high proportion of short term maturities. The existence of puts compounds the problem for issuers, but makes the market even more attractive for investors. On many Japanese issues, for example, the first put is no more than two and a half years from issue date. This makes Japanese Swiss franc convertibles extremely attractive for investors, because of the very limited downside risk.

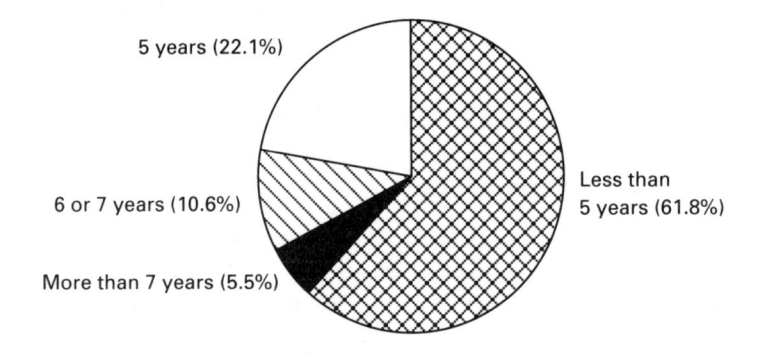

5 years (22.1%)
6 or 7 years (10.6%)
More than 7 years (5.5%)
Less than 5 years (61.8%)

Exhibit 13.12 New issue volume analysed by maturity in the Swiss convertible market in 1988

Coupon

Because Swiss franc interest rates are low by international standards, coupons on convertibles are low. For example, in the last few years, there have been many Japanese convertibles with coupons as low as ¼%. In some exceptional cases, the coupon has been zero. No other market in the world offers such consistently low coupons.

For non-Japanese companies willing to assume the Swiss franc currency risk, a Swiss franc convertible can be particularly attractive because the coupon is often below the dividend yield on the underlying stock. This can be advantageous if the convertible is converted, for not only will the shares on conversion have been issued at a higher price than would have been possible with a straight equity issue, but also, in the period before conversion, the cash flow cost of servicing the convertible will have been lower than the cost of paying dividends on the underlying shares (assuming no adverse exchange rate movements).

Conversion premium

For Japanese issuers, the conversion premium is the standard 5% customary in the Japanese market. For non-Japanese issuers, premiums typically vary between 15 and 20%, although in some exceptional cases (very well-known Swiss blue-chip companies for example), the premium might be as high as 30%. As a general rule, the premiums available to issuers are lower than would be possible in the Euromarket or the US domestic market.

Early redemption features

Issuer's optional redemption

Like their Euromarket and US domestic counterparts, Swiss franc convertibles are either non-callable from the outset for a short period (up to half the lifetime of the issue) or callable only if the share price appreciates to predetermined trigger levels (provisional call). One difference between Swiss franc convertibles and their Euromarket and US domestic counterparts is that the provisional call facility, called an acceleration clause in Switzerland, can sometimes be expressed in terms of the secondary market bond price, rather than the share price. For example, the issuer can accelerate conversion when the bonds reach 150% of issue price. In contrast, in the Euromarket and US domestic market, the trigger is always determined by reference to the underlying share price. This difference has no practical effect, for in both cases investors have significant upside potential before the call can be effected.

Investor's optional redemption

Many Swiss franc convertibles offer the investor a one-time

option to redeem the bonds early at a premium to their issue price. The yield to put would be equivalent to 50 to 75% of the yield which the company's straight (non-convertible) Swiss franc bonds might require. If offered, the put is usually available within a very short period of launch, typically within two to four years.

Investors

Swiss banking rules relating to secrecy make it difficult to ascertain much about the investor base in Swiss franc convertibles. What is known, however, is that in addition to indigenous Swiss individual and institutional investors, a large proportion of the funds invested in Swiss franc convertibles are provided by non-Swiss entities, either very wealthy private individuals or foreign institutions with a portion of their portfolios managed on a discretionary basis by the Swiss private banks.

Swiss individual and institutional investors are not significantly different from their counterparts in, for example, the United States or the United Kingdom, although many market participants believe retail (individual) investment in the Swiss market is a higher component of overall demand for convertibles than would be the case in the United States or the United Kingdom. Swiss insurance companies, pension funds, and private banks acting on behalf of their discretionary funds under management are believed to be the predominant institutional buyers. Unlike the US market or Euromarket, there are relatively few dedicted convertible investors, i.e. institutions or portfolio managers whose sole mandate is to invest exclusively in convertibles.

Regulations governing new issues

There are two types of convertible issue: a public offering and a private placement. Swiss National Bank regulations require that both must be lead managed by a Swiss-domiciled bank and that the syndicate be composed of Swiss-domiciled firms. The difference between the two types of issue is that a private placement is distributed primarily to the lead manager's in-house fund managers, is offered in denominations of SF50,000 and is not usually listed; a public issue on the other hand is offered publicly throughout Switzerland in denominations of SF5,000 and SF50,000 and is listed on most, if not all, of the principal Swiss stock exchanges. Approximately 60% of outstanding issues are private placements; the balance are public bond issues.

Disclosure requirements are the same for both types of offering and are relatively straightforward. There is no Swiss equivalent of the US SEC and no requirement to prepare financial statements in accordance with Swiss Generally Accepted Accounting Principles (GAAP). The level of disclosure acceptable in the issuer's home country is usually equally acceptable in Switzerland, with minor modifications. On a public issue the lead manager will prepare prospectus translations in French and German, as well as an English version, and publish an abridged version in three Swiss national newspapers. Permission of the Swiss National Bank is required for any Swiss franc issue; this is usually a formality obtained by the lead manager just prior to launch. Stock Exchange consents are also necessary for listing a public issue – again these are usually a formality and are handled by the lead manager.

Trading and settlement

Most issues are traded either on one of the official exchanges (in the case of public listed bond issues) or 'over-the-counter' via the telephone (primarily, although not exclusively, in the case of private unlisted note issues). In addition to official exchange prices, most of the principal market makers show prices 'live' on screen-based systems such as Reuters. Prices shown are usually good for dealing in size of up to SF250,000 face amount of bonds. As with other major convertible markets, the price quoted does not include accrued interest, which must be added to the agreed price on the basis of the number of days elapsed in a year of 360 days comprised of twelve 30 day months. Swiss franc convertibles are generally less liquid than their counterparts in other markets. The most liquid issues trade on a one point spread for a dealing size of SF250,000 (approximately US$150,000). Commissions are usually negotiable on large trades of SF250,000 or more. For smaller trades than this, dealers usually operate a fixed commission schedule. Settlement is usually book entry via SEGA, the Swiss National Securities Clearing System, and occurs seven calendar days from trade date.

Chapter 14

❖

Overview of the Japanese domestic market

The purpose of this chapter is to provide an overview of the convertible market in Japan; the principal issuers, the major investors, the types of convertible issued, and standard trading and settlement procedures. Whether measured by size or quality, the Japanese market is unique. Not only is it the biggest market in the world, by a fairly large margin, but it is also one of the highest quality markets, in that many of Japan's largest and most prestigious blue-chip companies are regular borrowers. No other market offers so much quality in depth.

Size of market

Exhibit 14.1 illustrates that the Japanese market is the largest convertible market in the world, being almost twice the size of its nearest counterpart, the US market. Part of the reason for this lies in the pattern of funding that Japanese companies have employed in recent years. Exhibit 14.2 illustrates that of the Y19.2 trillion ($140 billion) raised by Japanese companies in fiscal 1988 (i.e. the year ending March 31 1989), almost 42% was in the form of convertibles. No other major industrialised nation makes such use of convertibles; indeed, in most Western economies, convertibles account for at most 5 to 10% of total corporate fund-raising activity.

Exhibit 14.3 illustrates the growth of the Japanese market in the last few years. New issue volume in fiscal 1988 was more than four times that of fiscal 1984. No other convertible market has grown as rapidly. There are a number of reasons for this, including:

1. The strength of the Japanese stock market over this period.

New issue volume in 1988

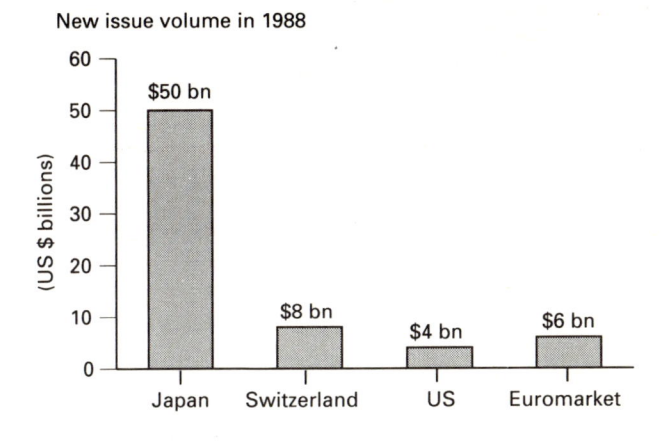

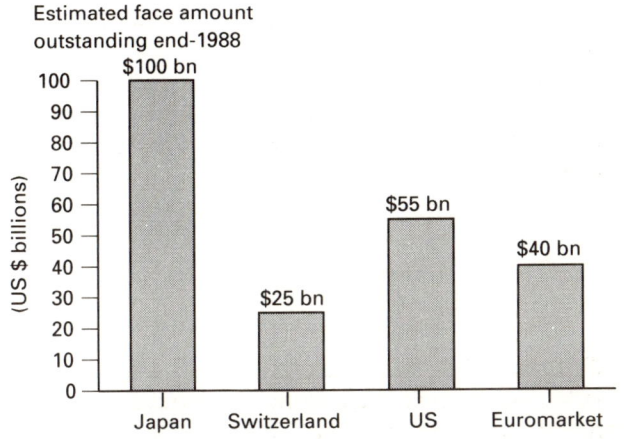

- Japan: $50 bn
- Switzerland: $8 bn
- US: $4 bn
- Euromarket: $6 bn

Estimated face amount outstanding end-1988

- Japan: $100 bn
- Switzerland: $25 bn
- US: $55 bn
- Euromarket: $40 bn

Exhibit 14.1 Comparison of the world's major convertible markets

Many Japanese corporations, which historically have operated with higher levels of debt to equity than their Western counterparts, took advantage of the rise in share prices over this period to raise fresh equity and strengthen their capital base. As Exhibit 14.2 illustrates, almost 92% of all fund-raising activity by Japanese companies in fiscal 1988 was in the form of equity or quasi equity, such as convertibles or bonds with warrants.

2. The more limited dilution that a convertible offers relative to an issue of shares. Since a convertible enables companies to issue shares at a premium (provided the convertible is converted), dilution in terms of earnings and ownership is lower for a convertible than for straight equity. Given the

Total: Yen 19,216 bn

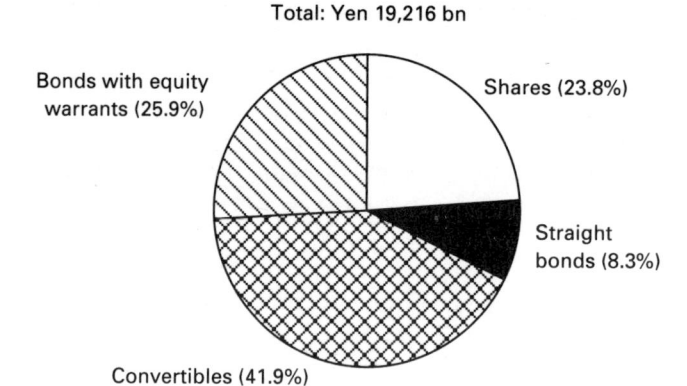

Bonds with equity warrants (25.9%)
Shares (23.8%)
Straight bonds (8.3%)
Convertibles (41.9%)

Exhibit 14.2 External financing by Japanese corporations in Japan and overseas in the Japanese convertible market in fiscal 1988 (*Source*: The Bond Underwriters Association of Japan)

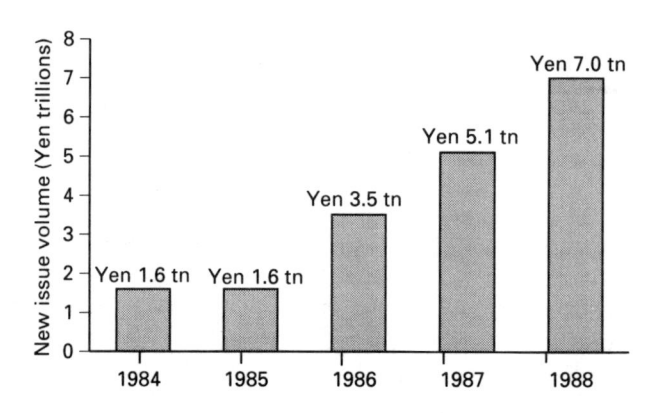

New issue volume (Yen trillions)
- 1984: Yen 1.6 tn
- 1985: Yen 1.6 tn
- 1986: Yen 3.5 tn
- 1987: Yen 5.1 tn
- 1988: Yen 7.0 tn

Exhibit 14.3 New issue volume in the Japanese convertible market in fiscal 1984–8 (*Source*: The Bond Underwriters Association of Japan)

virtual certainty of conversion of Japanese convertibles (conversion premiums are typically just 5%), a convertible financing is a more attractive method of raising equity for Japanese companies than issuing shares.

3. A more liberal regulatory environment. Unsecured convertible bond issues were prohibited until as recently as 1979 when the first such issue, for Matsushita, was floated. Since then, as the Japanese capital markets have matured, the Japanese Ministry of Finance ('MoF'), which regulates public offerings in Japan in much the same way as the SEC does in the United

States, has eased the restrictions on the issue of securities such as convertibles and bonds with equity warrants, with the results seen today.
4. Strong investor demand for convertibles, fuelled partly by the strength in the stock market, and partly by the greater liquidity of convertibles than their underlying shares. Exhibit 14.4 illustrates the latter point: although the market capitalisation of all convertible issues is only 3% of the combined stock and convertible market capitalisation, trading activity in convertibles accounts for 20% of combined trading activity, with the result that convertibles are more liquid than shares, and therefore more attractive to investors, all other things being equal.

Issuer profile

One of the hallmarks of the Japanese market is the high quality of the borrowers. Most, if not all, of Japan's major blue-chip companies have made use of the convertible market at one point or another, as Exhibit 14.5 illustrates. This is in direct contrast to the position in, for example, the United States, where convertibles are still regarded by many as appropriate only for lesser quality credits, and where the number of blue-chip corporations accessing the market is fairly limited.

Another attraction for investors of the Japanese market is that most sectors of the economy are well represented, as Exhibit 14.6 illustrates. There is a broad spread of investing opportunities, with issues from basic industrial companies, car, food and consumer products companies, the financial services sector and electric utilities. Only the US market offers a comparable spread of investing opportunities.

Largest issues

The largest ever issues in the Japanese market are presented in Exhibit 14.7. Although the record for the largest ever convertible offering worldwide is held by a US company in the US market (Time Warner, with a $5.3 billion convertible preferred offering), the Japanese market offers more issues of a larger size than any other market. Eight of the issues listed in Exhibit 14.7 exceed $1 billion in size.

Market capitalisation of outstanding issues at end 1988

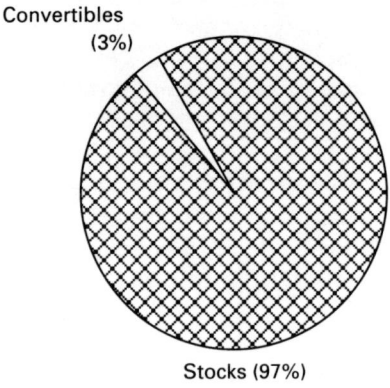

Convertibles (3%)

Stocks (97%)
(TSE 1st and 2nd sections)

Total: Yen 493 trillion

Market value of trading activity in 1988

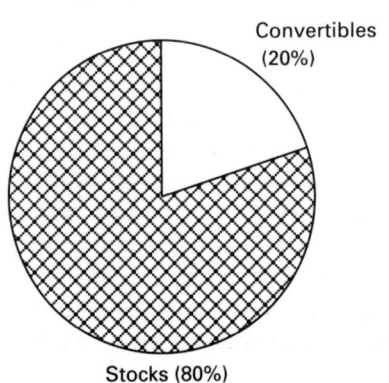

Convertibles (20%)

Stocks (80%)
(TSE 1st and 2nd sections)

Total: Yen 356 trillion

Exhibit 14.4 Secondary market size and trading volumes in the Japanese convertible market (*Source*: Tokyo Stock Exchange)

Foreign issuers

There has only been one non-Japanese offering in the Japanese market so far: a $175 million issue in 1989 from P&O, the UK

Date	Issuer	Amount raised
Oct. 1989	Asahi Chemical	Y 80bn
Jul. 1984	Canon	Y 50bn
May 1989	Hitachi	Y250bn
Aug. 1988	Kirin Brewery	Y 50bn
May 1987	Matsushita	Y200bn
Mar. 1989	Mazda	Y100bn
Aug. 1986	Mitsubishi Heavy Industries	Y100bn
Mar. 1988	Mitsui & Co	Y 50bn
Oct. 1988	NEC	Y120bn
Jul. 1989	NKK	Y 70bn
Jun. 1989	Nippon Steel	Y100bn
Dec. 1987	Nissan	Y100bn
Oct. 1987	Sanyo	Y 60bn
Apr. 1987	Sharp	Y 70bn
Apr. 1988	Sony	Y 92bn
May 1988	Sumitomo Bank	Y 75bn
May 1988	Tokyo Marine & Fire	Y 50bn
Jan. 1989	Tokyo Electric Power	Y180bn
Nov. 1989	Toshiba	Y150bn
Jul. 1988	Toyota	Y300bn

Exhibit 14.5 Selected issuers in the Japanese convertible market 1984–9

company. It is possible that there could be more such issues, because many Western companies have a strategic objective of increasing their Japanese investor base, and a Japanese convertible represents an attractive method of achieving this objective without the reflow risks associated with an issue of ordinary shares. (Japanese investors have a somewhat patchy track record of holding onto shares issued by Western companies in the Japanese domestic market – many such offerings have quickly reflowed back to the home market soon after issue date.) However, several structural obstacles to further issuance remain:

1. The low conversion premium typical of Japanese convertibles. Japanese investors are accustomed to investing in convertibles with a 5% conversion premium. Western companies, on the other hand, are accustomed to issuing convertibles with premiums in the 15 to 30% range. Japanese investors are reluctant to purchase convertibles with Western style conversion premiums; equally, Western companies are reluctant to issue convertibles with conversion premiums as low as 5%. The compromise adopted by P&O (a 15% premium) met with limited success.

1985
Total: Yen 1,586 bn

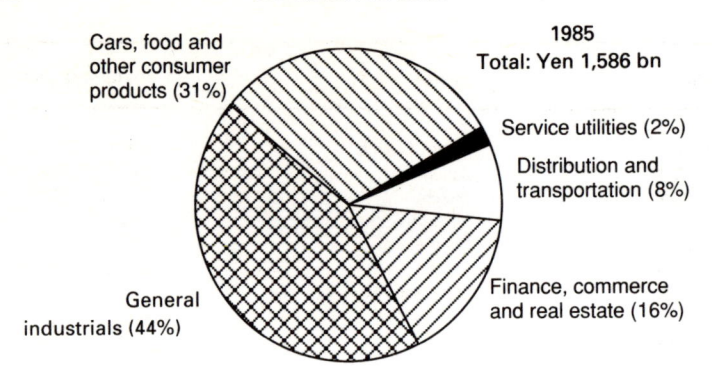

- Cars, food and other consumer products (31%)
- Service utilities (2%)
- Distribution and transportation (8%)
- Finance, commerce and real estate (16%)
- General industrials (44%)

1986
Total: Yen 3,468 bn

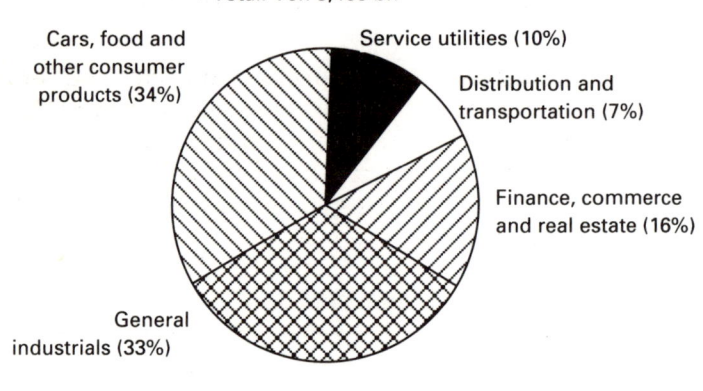

- Cars, food and other consumer products (34%)
- Service utilities (10%)
- Distribution and transportation (7%)
- Finance, commerce and real estate (16%)
- General industrials (33%)

1987
Total: Yen 5.055 bn

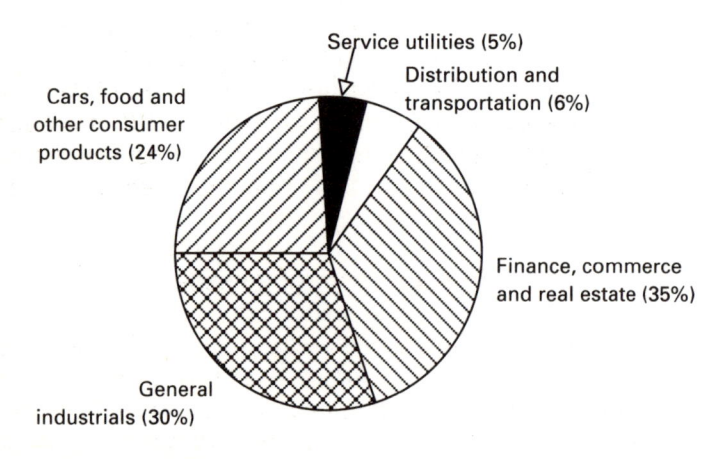

- Cars, food and other consumer products (24%)
- Service utilities (5%)
- Distribution and transportation (6%)
- Finance, commerce and real estate (35%)
- General industrials (30%)

Exhibit 14.6 Issue volume analysed by type of issuer in the Japanese convertible market in fiscal 1985–7

Date	Issuer	Amount raised
Jul. 1988	Toyota	Y300bn
May 1989	Hitachi	Y250bn
Dec. 1986	Toyota	Y200bn
May 1987	Matsushita	Y200bn
Oct. 1989	Matsushita	Y200bn
Jan. 1989	Tokyo Electric Power	Y180bn
Oct. 1989	Mitsui Real Estate	Y150bn
Nov. 1989	Toshiba	Y150bn
Jan. 1987	Hitachi	Y120bn
Aug. 1988	Hitachi	Y120bn
Oct. 1988	NEC	Y120bn

Exhibit 14.7 Largest issues in the Japanese convertible market

2. The currency risk of issuing a yen denominated security. Japanese investors prefer yen denominated convertibles, but Western companies are reluctant to incur the currency risk of a yen denominated exposure. A 'half-way house' compromise may be a US dollar denominated issue (such as was offered by P&O), but this has less appeal to Japanese investors, and with the exception of US companies, is less than ideal for Western issuers.
3. Various regulatory and other requirements imposed by the Japanese MoF and the securities industry. The MoF tightly regulates all public offerings in Japan and requires, among other things, that any prospective foreign convertible issuer prepare a prospectus in Japanese. In addition, the securities industry has established minimum qualification standards for a public offering which include, among other things, that any foreign issuer have its shares listed on the Tokyo Stock Exchange and be rated single A or better (BBB if net assets exceed Y33 billion ($250 million)). Not all prospective convertible issuers from the West can meet these requirements.

Typical convertible issue

In Japan, there is only one type of convertible: a conventional convertible bond. Convertible preferreds, or convertible bond structures such as zeros and premium puts, are unknown in the Japanese market, even though Japanese corporations are fairly regular issuers of these instruments elsewhere (e.g. in the Swiss market).

Average size

The size of the average convertible offering has almost doubled in the last five years to Y21.0 billion ($150 million), as Exhibit 14.8 illustrates. In common with other major convertible markets, Japanese investors have shown a marked preference in the last few years for larger more liquid issues, on the basis that these are more tradeable than their smaller counterparts, and therefore offer the investor greater protection if stock markets decline. At Y21.0 billion, Japanese convertible issues are larger, on average, than their Western counterparts.

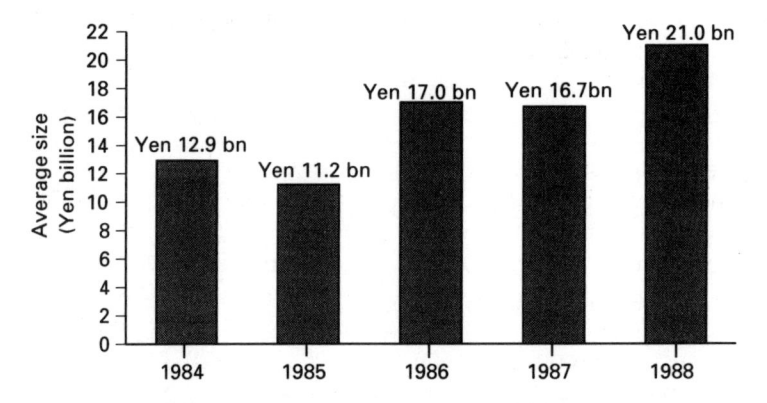

Exhibit 14.8 Average size of new issues in the Japanese convertible market in fiscal 1984–8

Maturity

Exhibit 14.9 illustrates the typical maturities of Japanese convertible issues. Most are ten years or shorter, although in recent years there has been a trend to longer dated issues, with the longest being fifteen years.

Coupon and conversion premium

As with other major convertible markets, coupons on Japanese convertibles are established somewhere between the dividend yield on the underlying shares and the yield on straight bonds of an equivalent maturity. The coupons are usually determined by

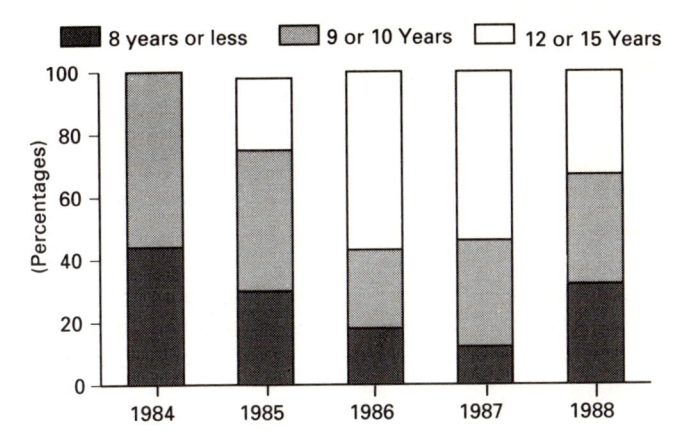

Exhibit 14.9 Issue volume analysed by maturity in the Japanese convertible market in fiscal 1984–8

reference to 'standard rates'. These are benchmark rates for pricing convertibles which are established by consensus within the securities industry and changed two times each month to reflect changes in secondary market trading levels. The standard rates are adjusted for each issue by the lead manager at its discretion to reflect specific differences from the benchmark in areas such as credit quality of the issuer, maturity of the issue, liquidity of the issue and underlying shares, etc.

Conversion premiums on Japanese convertibles are nearly always 5%, by custom. Although there is no law requiring this, there is strong investor resistance to higher premiums. One of the very few exceptions to the 5% norm so far was the issue by P&O, which offered a 15% premium. Coupons are paid semi-annually and are subject to a 20% withholding tax.

Early redemption features

Convertibles are typically callable for early redemption by the issuer at any time, starting halfway to final maturity. Thus for example, a ten year issue would be callable from the end of year five onwards, while a twelve year issue would be callable from the end of year six onwards. There is usually a modest premium which the issuer must pay to effect the call, although this declines over time to zero by final maturity, and in any event is hardly ever paid, because most issues are converted before they are called. Investor put options and sinking funds are rare, although the latter used to be fairly common.

Investor profile

There is a major difference between where convertibles are initially placed (primary market), and where they eventually end up being held (secondary market), as Exhibits 14.10, 14.11 and 14.12 illustrate. The Tokyo Stock Exchange requires that for a new convertible issue to be listed, a major proportion of the issue should be placed with individual (retail) and corporate investors, rather than institutions. This accounts for the profile of primary market investment activity illustrated in Exhibit 14.10, which shows that almost 83% of all new convertible issues in fiscal 1988 were placed initially with corporations and individuals.

However, neither Japanese retail nor corporate investors are the most natural long-term holders of convertibles, with the result that they have both been significant net sellers in the secondary market, as is illustrated in Exhibit 14.11. Exhibit 14.11 also illustrates that the major net purchasers of convertibles in the last few years were the securities firms for their own account (mostly arbitrage related activity) and to a lesser extent, investment trusts. Notwithstanding this, there is considerable turnover of convertibles in the secondary market, as Exhibit 14.4 illustrates, and convertibles can pass through many hands before reaching their final 'homes', as Exhibit 14.12 illustrates.

The trading activities of the trust banks illustrated in Exhibit 14.12 are of particular interest. Although the trust banks have not

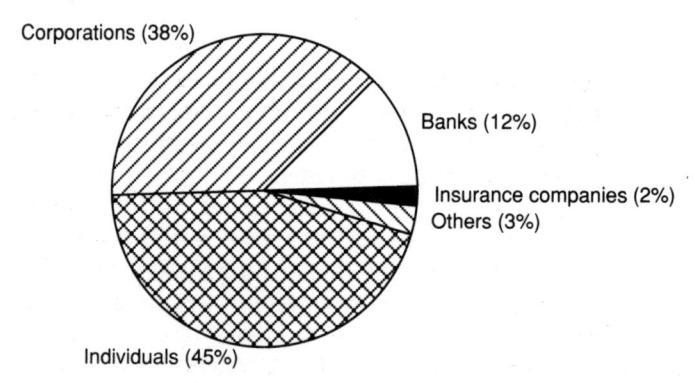

Exhibit 14.10 Primary market investors in new issues in the Japanese convertible market in fiscal 1988 (*Source*: The Bond Underwriters Association of Japan)

	1986	1987 Y billion	1988
Securities firms' own account	872	(932)	(5,969)
Banks	(623)	(26)	796
Corporations	(191)	568	2,669
Individuals	583	1,118	1,822
Investment trusts	(260)	(936)	(405)
Foreigners	(61)	139	534
Insurance companies	12	(42)	77
Others	8	119	444

Exhibit 14.11 Analysis of secondary market sales (purchases) by type of investor in the Japanese convertible market in fiscal 1986–8 (*Source*: Tokyo Stock Exchange)

been significant purchasers in the primary market, nor significant net purchasers in the secondary market, their trading activity in convertibles exceeds that of all other categories of investor, with the exception of the securities firms themselves. Trading by trust banks has grown significantly in the last few years, mostly as a result of growth in Tokkin funds, which are short term investment vehicles set up by the trust banks and used by companies and others for managing surplus cash.

Trading and settlement

As is illustrated in Exhibit 14.4, convertibles are usually more liquid than their underlying shares, for at least three reasons:

1. The differences between the primary and secondary markets outlined above, which necessitates considerable trading activity before convertibles reach their final investment 'home' from where they are initially placed.
2. The lack of interlinking cross shareholdings on convertibles. There are significant cross shareholdings between companies and banks in Japan, reflecting business groupings such as *zaibatsus*. These cross shareholdings are permanent and never trade, so that the free 'float' of shares available for trading is significantly lower than the total number of shares in issue. This, in turn, reduces overall trading liquidity. There are no such cross-holdings on convertibles and therefore no impairments to secondary market liquidity.

THE PRINCIPAL MARKETS

Overall market
Total: Yen 43,400 bn face value

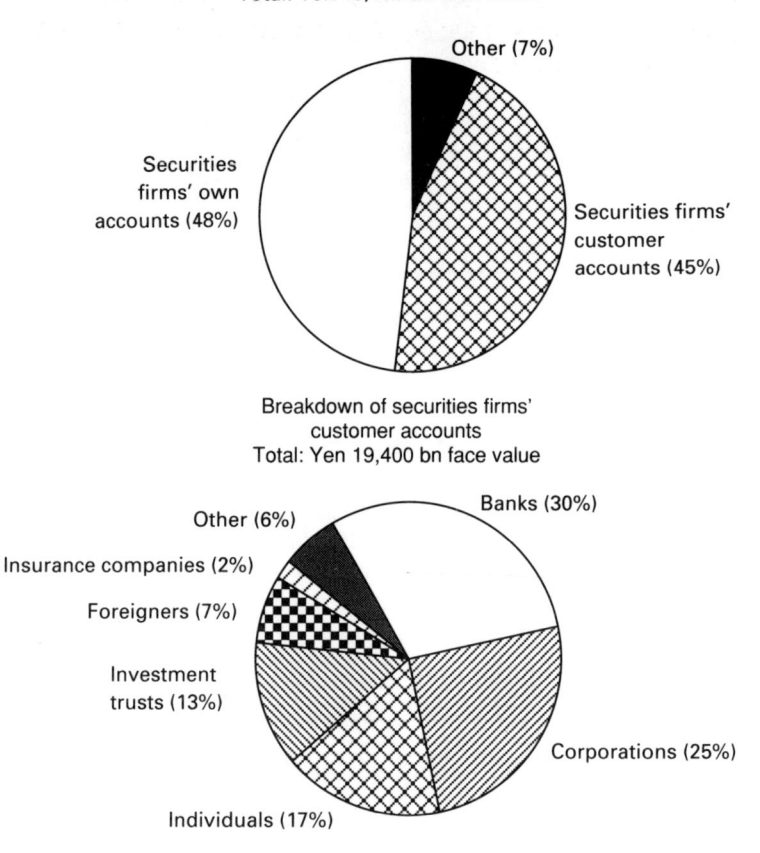

- Other (7%)
- Securities firms' own accounts (48%)
- Securities firms' customer accounts (45%)

Breakdown of securities firms' customer accounts
Total: Yen 19,400 bn face value

- Banks (30%)
- Other (6%)
- Insurance companies (2%)
- Foreigners (7%)
- Investment trusts (13%)
- Individuals (17%)
- Corporations (25%)

Exhibit 14.12 Breakdown of secondary market trading activity by type of investor in the Japanese convertible market in fiscal 1988 (*Source*: Tokyo Stock Exchange)

3. Lower commission structures on convertibles. Commissions are fixed in Japan for trading in both convertibles and ordinary shares: the cost of commissions and transfer taxes in convertibles is generally 70–80% of that on shares.

All convertibles are exchange traded, primarily on the Tokyo Stock Exchange, but also to a lesser extent on the Osaka and Nagoya exchanges. Regular way settlement, accounting for more than 95% of all trades, occurs three business days after trade date.

Physical delivery versus payment is the standard method of settlement. Accrued interest is added to the agreed price, and calculated on the basis of the number of days elapsed in a year of 365 days, less 20% withholding tax.

Glossary

❖

Absolute call	A convertible with an absolute call can be redeemed for early redemption by the issuer at any time under any circumstance (i.e. without pre-condition) during the absolute call period.
Adjusted breakeven	Breakeven calculated according to the following formula: $$\frac{\text{Market value of convertible (\%)} - \text{Parity value (\%)}}{\text{Market value of convertible (\%)} \times \text{coupon (\%)} - \text{Parity value (\%)} \times \text{stock yield (\%)}}$$
Billion	1,000 million
Bond premium	The difference between the market value of the convertible and its bond value.
Bond value (or investment value)	The value of the convertible as a straight bond without the conversion option.
Breakeven (or payback)	The number of years it takes for the stock investor to recoup the conversion premium (extra cost of buying the convertible rather than the stock) from the convertible's higher income.
Call	An option, exercisable by the company, to redeem the convertible prior to final maturity.

GLOSSARY

Conversion premium	The difference between the market value of the convertible and its parity value, usually expressed as a percentage of parity value.
Conversion price	The price per share at which the convertible can be converted into shares of common stock.
Conversion ratio	The number of shares of common stock into which each convertible can be converted.
Conversion value	Same as *Parity value*.
Convertible bonds (or debentures)	Debt securities issued by a company that are convertible at the investor's option into shares of common stock of the company.
Convertible debentures	Same as *Convertible bonds*.
Convertible preferreds	Preferred shares issued by a company that are convertible at the investor's option into shares of common stock of the company.
Discounted income advantage	The present value of the difference between the convertible's coupon and the underlying stock's yield, discounted over the period until the stock's dividend exceeds the coupon on the convertible for the first time.
Exchangeable	A convertible issued by the company that can be converted into another company's shares, rather than its own. In the United States, exchangeable can have another meaning, namely the right of an issuer, if so stated, to exchange its existing convertible preferreds for convertible debentures with identical terms.

GLOSSARY

Flexible put convertible — A rolling premium put convertible in which the issuer establishes the price and date of just the first put option at the convertible's original issue date. The terms of each succeeding put are established just prior to the preceding put, in order to give the issuer maximum flexibility to reflect changes in market conditions between the put dates.

Hard call — A convertible with a hard call is not callable for early redemption by the issuer under any circumstance during the hard call period.

Investment value — Same as *Bond value*.

Low premium convertible — A convertible issued or trading with a low conversion premium and low coupon to match.

LYON — A type of zero coupon convertible. Short for Liquid Yield Option Note.

Par — The redemption value of the convertible as a bond at final maturity.

Par put convertible — A convertible in which the investor has a put option prior to final maturity, and the price of the put is at par.

Parity value (stock value or conversion value) — The market value of the shares of common stock into which the convertible can be converted.

Payback — Same as *Breakeven*.

Premium put convertible — A convertible in which the investor has a put option prior to final maturity, and the price of the put is at a premium to par.

GLOSSARY

Provisional call	A convertible with a provisional call is callable for early redemption by the issuer during the provisional call period, but only if the issuer's share price is above a predetermined premium to the conversion price.
Put	An option, exerciseable by the investor, to redeem the convertible prior to final maturity.
Rolling premium put convertible	A premium put convertible with several premium put options. Typically, each put option is structured in such a way that on any put date, the terms of the next put are sufficiently attractive that the investor has an economic incentive to continue holding the convertible until the next put date, rather than exercise the put. In this way the convertible should remain outstanding until final maturity or until it is converted.
Simple breakeven	Breakeven calculated according to the following formula: $$\frac{\text{Market value of convertible (\%)} - \text{Parity value (\%)}}{\text{Convertible coupon (\%)} - \text{Stock yield (\%)}}$$
Stock value	Same as *Parity value*.
Trillion	1,000 billion
Zero coupon convertible	A convertible without a coupon.

Index

bond premium 7, 80, 88–92
bond value 7, 69, 71–3, 80, 88, 91–3, 95
breakeven 49, 50, 79, 128
   adjusted 82–5, 87
   simple 82–3, 87
business and financial distress, impact of 7, 72–3, 93
   events of default 4
   liquidation rights 4

call options 5, 23, 25, 28, 33–5, 40, 50, 60–2, 64, 75, 95, 111, 129, 143
conventional convertible 10, 15–19, 22, 25–31, 43, 49, 59, 61–2, 66, 68, 80, 99, 128–9, 135
conversion premium 5, 10, 20, 22, 29–30, 33, 36–7, 49, 50, 54, 59–64, 71, 110, 119, 128, 143, 148, 151, 154–5
conversion price 8–9, 16–17, 20–1, 23–5, 27–31, 33, 37, 43, 54, 80, 111
conversion ratio 5, 8–10, 24, 27–9, 37, 81, 87
conversion value 9
convertible bond 3, 11, 59, 119, 129, 148, 153
convertible preferred 3, 4, 11, 59, 120, 124, 127–9, 149, 153
cost of capital 18, 19, 26
currency and interest swaps 40–1, 136–7

discounted income advantage 79, 82, 85–7

equity warrants 38–43, 56–7, 89–92, 99–101, 120, 135–6, 138, 147, 149
event risk 5

interest rates, impact of 48, 57, 69–70, 76, 94
investment value 7

low premium convertible 10, 22–5, 59–61, 66
LYON 11, 36, 63

par 3, 7–8, 24, 27, 30, 36–7, 51, 68, 72–5, 80, 85, 87, 95, 111, 129
parity value 9, 10, 54, 70, 73, 79–87, 91–5, 112
payback 49, 50, 82
premium put convertible 5, 9, 11, 59–63, 67, 99, 101, 111, 113, 120, 129, 135, 137, 153
   flexible premium put 11, 32, 62, 101, 113
   rolling premium put 11, 15–17, 22, 27–36, 43, 62, 101, 113
   single premium put 11, 15, 20–2, 34–6, 43

rule 144A 117, 125

stock value 9

takeover, impact of 48, 57, 70–1, 76, 94
trading, liquidity and settlement 48, 57, 71–2, 75–6, 94, 116, 130–1, 145, 157–9

zero coupon convertible 3, 11, 15, 20–3, 36–8, 43, 57, 59, 63–5, 120–1, 128–9, 153